Just the Right Words:
201 Report Card Comments

Short Narrative Comments, Word Lists, and Sentence Starters That Cover Any Situation, Let Parents Know How Their Kids Are Doing—and Save You Time!

by Mona Melwani

NEW YORK • TORONTO • LONDON • AUCKLAND • SYDNEY
MEXICO CITY • NEW DELHI • HONG KONG • BUENOS AIRES

SCHOLASTIC
Teaching
Resources

ACKNOWLEDGMENTS

This book evolved out of the camaraderie shared with my colleagues at Taipei American School, Taipei, Taiwan.

When I decided to leave teaching, the thought that gave me the most relief was no longer having to write report cards and narratives. Every time report card writing time had approached, I felt my responsibility as a teacher to be the heaviest. In my estimation, my evaluations had to be as fair as King Solomon.

Although I realized I might be making the task larger than it really was, I also knew objectively that this was a critical moment in the instructional process. Even when I was no longer in the classroom, report card writing continued to fill my thoughts. I knew I would have to confront it head-on. So, rather than turning away from it, I decided to immerse myself in it. And this book is the result.

I owe an enormous debt of gratitude to Taipei American School, where every teacher is a mentor and every administrator fine-tunes this excellence, creating opportunities for personal and professional growth beyond expectation. There are too many teachers and administrators, spread over the seventeen years I taught at the school, to thank by name; they created the caring and conscientious environment that me feel that fair and justifiable evaluation was an absolute expectation of good instruction.

I would like to thank Wendy Murray and Joanna Davis-Swing at Scholastic for their encouragement and advice. I could not have asked for a better editor than Merryl Maleska Wilbur. Merryl suggested perspectives that made me reflect. I am sure that the additions that grew from our interaction have increased the usefulness of my book.

As usual, the person who gets relegated 'to last but not least' is the most important. My utmost gratitude must go to my husband, Murli—my inspiration and my encouragement, who bore my despair and translated my feelings and thoughts into this constructive whole.

Cover design by Maria Lilja
Cover photo © Dennis MacDonald/Photo Edit Inc.
Interior design by Solutions by Design, Inc.
Interior Photo Credits: p.6: Dennis MacDonald/Photo Edit Inc.;
p.22: Tom Hurst via SODA; p.38: James Levin/Studio 10/SODA;
p.54: Photodisc via SODA; p.66 & 76: Richard Hutchings via SODA

ISBN: 0-439-53136-5

Copyright © 2003 by Mona Melwani
All rights reserved. Printed in the USA.

4 5 6 7 8 9 10   40   09 08 07 06 05 04

Table of Contents

Introduction

The inspiration for this book springs from my experience as a teacher in international schools for almost twenty years. As my colleagues and I struggled every quarter, tussling with words and fashioning them to fit the umpteen situations and personalities in the classroom, I recognized some basic uncertainties that teachers go through. There is the dread of:

- being repetitive
- being verbose
- not saying enough
- saying too much
- discovering that one has actually said nothing at all.

There is no lack of information that teachers have available on each student; the difficulty lies instead in how to sift through that information and choose those aspects that will be the most constructive to focus on.

I realize that the acclaimed international school in Asia in which I taught is atypical, if not unique— an American school set in Asia with a student body representing over fifty countries. Its Asian context means that the school is invested with the singularly dynamic quality that Asian culture brings to education. The students I taught were exceptionally well behaved and compelled to do their best by expectations at home. The pressures on both teachers and students were intense. In these respects, my teaching experience was quite unusual.

Nonetheless, I believe that key universal goals and challenges link teachers around the globe. My experience was with lower primary grades, where the children are vulnerable and the parents sensitive. The dilemma is to say what one has to, to not 'sugar the pill,' and yet to articulate the message in a productive way. I believe it is vital for teachers to approach the task with this core question in mind, "What must Michael focus on now that will be the most helpful to him?" To do this thoroughly usually means a teacher must go through the data many times over in order to etch in a full and fair composite picture.

The pressures of a regular teaching day and the units of study that must be completed within rigorous timeframes, coupled with the task of writing perceptive and fair report cards, can be exhausting. The squeeze on time means that teachers spend long days and weekends keeping up with schoolwork. Nonetheless, there is a bright side to this.

There is a special camaraderie that builds among teachers during these stressful times. We realize that 'we are all in it together.' The report card-related exchanges that take place in our quiet after-school classrooms nurture, I believe, impressive professional development. Dropping into each other's rooms and becoming peer editors for the moment—going through each other's work for punctuation, for clarity, for tips on 'how can I say this better?'—make us realize just how much a second opinion helps.

For example, a colleague who's running low on word-steam might come in and sigh, "I have a kid who just can't seem to settle down, get started, and get moving. He's here, there, and everywhere, and never gets his work finished. Yet, if I hover around him like a policeman he can work straight through. How do I say all this on the report card?"

Well, she's said it well enough, hasn't she— but she's not happy with that. As a teacher yourself, you know that it's she who can't seem to settle down about how to comment on this child. So you ask, "Tell me more about this kid. I have a student like that too." And you wind up talking through the process until she's comfortable. It is in this circle of kind support that teachers learn to convey the idea that 'Cindy is doing okay in math' articulately and in the specific, illuminating detail that is fair to the student.

My hope is that this book will provide you with that kind of support so that your report card writing becomes easier and better and so that you will have a helpful resource during what can be the most stressful times of the year.

How to Use This Book

There are over two hundred report card messages that can be drawn on instantly in this book. These ready-to-use comments are intended to help you, the classroom teacher, as you sit down to write your report cards. The hope is that as you deliberate on how to frame a particular thought or structure a certain sentence, you may find just what you need in the comments.

You might use a narrative just as it is, or you might want to select appropriate sentences and weave those into your own report. Or, alternately, you might choose excerpts from a number of narratives and put them together. You also might find that by reading a set of these comments and stepping back for a moment, your own phrasing clicks into place. All that is needed is the blending of all of these parts into the desired whole.

Chapters 2, 3, and 4 are organized by subject matter; each contains sections with narratives for students at various levels of academic strengths. Chapter 5 covers social-emotional behavior and work habits. Chapter 6 offers general comments that homeroom teachers may find especially appropriate. Finally, you'll find numerous appendices devoted to, among other things, sentence stems, verb choice, and helpful phrasings. These should, we hope, operate as expedient time savers for you.

One further note is in order. At the beginning of each chapter, you'll find a student profile and a report card with a narrative for that student. These are much like the portrait of Elizabeth in this chapter, although briefer. The profiles are created from the teacher's data collection, which includes scoring rubrics, writing inventory continuums, observations, student work, tests, and more. All of the samples are intended to show how the narrative comments correlate with the reported grade. Each point is made succinctly and meant to explain the grade against the student's performance. It's important to realize that the profiles do not follow a consistent format, but have been deliberately varied to allow for the fact that teachers use different modes and methods of assessment, and frequently adapt the design of their instruments to better align with their purposes. Thus, if some aspects of these profiles and report cards seem inconsistent across the chapter samples, that's not only fine, but deliberate.

I trust you will find your own individual way to make use of the comments that follow. The report card writing task may, I hope, prove less daunting with this book in hand.

CHAPTER 1

Report Cards Are an Important Communication Tool

REPORT CARDS ARE ONE OF THE MOST IMPORTANT communication tools a teacher has. Not only do they inform parents about their child's development in school, but they help students themselves monitor their learning progress. Every teacher has to write them two or three or four times a year, and no matter how long you've been teaching, report-card writing is not painless. It is my hope that this book will make the task easier, and that it will reduce the time you spend on writing report card comments.

Over the years, the format of the report card has changed considerably, but the narrative—the comments that support the grade marks on the report card—has remained more or less the same. This first chapter looks at the whole of the report card, but the focus of subsequent chapters of this book is on those narrative comments. At the end of this chapter, you'll find a section on how best to make use of the narratives.

Parents want the good news and the bad news about their child's growth. They tend to be focused on academic performance rather than behavioral standards. Therefore, it is part of the teacher's job to educate parents about the importance of both.

Perhaps not surprisingly, parents are also frequently concerned with their child's standing in his or her class. The simple question, "How well is my child doing?" may be a veiled inquiry into what parents most want to know: "How well is my child performing compared to others?" And while the parent may be more interested in that comparison, a teacher is often more concerned with other criteria in considering a child's performance, including:

- ✔ Grade level expectations
- ✔ Teacher expectations
- ✔ The child's ability

Parents learn a great deal about their children from teachers, so what we tell them must be supported with concrete examples. Both the task of collecting these examples and the task of evaluating them are significant undertakings. Depending on memory alone for these tasks is unreasonable and unreliable. Instead, it's a good idea to rely on quick and efficient tools such as sticky notes, checklists, and anecdotal records. It is especially helpful to allocate a fixed amount of time each day to recording your observations. Then, when it's time to begin writing report-card narratives, your job will be greatly streamlined.

Being honest and fair about assessment, and communicating that assessment effectively, are the core goals of writing a good report card. But the data also provide critical information for the teacher about herself. They compel the teacher to reflect on her teaching and assess how well the assignments fit the objectives. Thus, the report card is not only an instrument for communicating the student's performance to parents, but it serves as a vital self-diagnostic tool that affects decisions about future teaching and learning experiences.

In summary, a report card is many things. A teacher's remarks must cover both academic and non-academic areas. These remarks must be concise and selective. The choice of words must be sensitive, honest, critical, supportive, and constructive—all at the same time. A report card is something a family might hold on to as a keepsake, so teachers must reflect long and hard before they put words to paper.

These kinds of considerations can seem a bit daunting for the novice teacher. But rest assured—you'll find that when you put in the advance work required to build a student profile, you will be well prepared to report a child's progress. And experience in observing the learning process, a growing understanding of the philosophy on which your school's report card is based, and sources such as this book will help you get a handle on this complex process. In the end, writing report cards will probably prove to be a satisfying experience—one that helps you understand your own teaching better.

Report Cards and the Assessment Process

Behind every effective report card is an effective assessment process. Establishing and maintaining this process requires constant management on the teacher's part.

Teachers in almost every classroom use checklists, anecdotal jottings, lists of curricular objectives, and performance recording tools to track their students' performance. Indeed, a dizzying array of both teacher-created and commercially-produced tools, instruments, and procedures are available to assess multiple intelligences, different modalities of learning, and particular units of study. However, as long as a few basic criteria are met—aligning the method and the purpose and maintaining consistency throughout the instruction/assessment process—authentic assessment is possible and achievable. And authentic assessment that leads to creating a composite picture of a student's performance is a necessary first step before an effective report card can be generated.

Whole books are devoted to the assessment process. Here we will simply take a glimpse at some basic terms and principles, changes in assessment that are reflected in report cards, and what students and teachers most want to know from the process and the report.

Some Basic Terms and Principles

Although common terms in the assessment arena can be used differently, "assessment process" is usually accepted as an umbrella phrase, incorporating the various phases of gathering and collecting data, interpreting it, and ultimately forming judgments or evaluations. Thus, the report card itself lies at the evaluation end of the process; it is the key evaluative tool for elementary school teachers.

One of the guiding principles of assessment is that the methods used and questions posed should reflect as closely as possible what you want students to learn. Yet another principle maintains that assessment is useful and effective only if the teacher considers a wide gamut of factors, including:

- Effort
- Attitude
- Class participation
- Assignment completion
- General progress
- Specific student successes
- Skill and strategy development
- Involvement in projects and performances

Most teachers will agree with both principles, and indeed both are useful. In primary school classrooms where the homeroom teacher is with the students for most of the day, there are more opportunities to observe students over a wider range of performance. Thus, the second principle is usually stressed more by these teachers. Content-area teachers who may see their students for an hour each day of the week or just three times a week usually feel that it's most important that assessment should reflect as closely as possible what you want students to learn—that is, specific content goals. Again, both principles are valid and will inform the effective report card.

Changes in Assessment

Assessment has changed over the years, and report cards have been modified to reflect the philosophy of the day. The adjustments in the way student progress is reported have ranged from assigning a grade with a number score (75%), to giving letter grades (A, B, F), to using checks and pluses—or even circles and triangles—at strategic points on a continuum.

Report cards have gone through several evolutionary cycles in recent decades. Not long ago, spelling, grammar, and punctuation were evaluated separately. Then the *holistic* way of looking at literacy, with its emphasis on teaching integrated units, as well as the phenomenal growth of writing and writing process instruction, relegated those separate items to the back burner. Now, schools are including these skills again within the context of writing under editing, revising, and proofreading. New topics of assessment also are evident in math (for example, math vocabulary), and in social studies, where technology is incorporated in the study skill of locating resources.

In addition, there are ongoing changes in assessment and evaluation practices. The result is that we have more tools to evaluate with, more areas to evaluate, and more controversies. The hottest of these conflicts center on the following:

- Grade marks versus no grade marks
- Portfolio assessment conferences versus standard parent-teacher conferences
- Narrative reports alone versus narrative comments along with grade marks

The methods of assessment constitute yet another arena of controversy and frequent change. Debates about the merits of each of the following topics are common:

- Pencil and paper tests

Just the Right Words: 201 Report Card Comments • Scholastic Teaching Resources

- Oral presentations
- Oral explanation as response to questions
- Tests requiring essay-type answers
- Objective tests: choosing among options
- Skills focus versus knowledge focus
- Use of portfolios to document growth

Throughout the changes and the controversies, at least one thing has remained constant: what parents and students would like to *learn* from the report card.

What Students and Parents Want to Know

In a random survey, I asked both students and parents what they would most like to learn from a report card. Following are their responses:

STUDENTS

- Am I doing well?
- How well am I doing?
- How am I doing compared to the rest of the students in class?
- Who is better than me in this class?
- Does the teacher like me?
- Do my classmates think I am stupid?

PARENTS
Parents want answers to all of the above questions, and they also want to know:

- Is my child intelligent or not?
- What's the highest score in class?
- Is my child well-behaved? Is my child obedient?
- How can I help my child reach the top of the class?

The survey also revealed that both parents and students think that the teacher knows best. This trust obligates us to be thorough, to be thoughtful, and to stay updated about educational and pedagogical issues.

Tools of the Trade: Report Card Components

Overview of the Report Card Structure

Report cards come in different sizes and formats. As already mentioned, the items to be scored have changed, and letter grades may have been replaced by checks and pluses. Generally, though, there are two standard elements of the report card structure. This section looks briefly at both of them. First, the report card employs a scale of **descriptors,** defined explicitly in terms of standardized criteria within a school district. Descriptors can take many forms across school districts, so the same descriptor (a checkmark or a term such as "developing," for instance) can stand for one thing in one district and something else in another.

Partially for this reason, the other element of the report card—the written set of comments called the **narrative**—is extremely important. It not only amplifies, but also clarifies, your report on the student's performance.

Report Card Descriptors

The following is a list of three sets of common descriptors used in different report cards, along with the definitions that accompany each descriptor on that report card. Varied though they are, some of them mean the same thing.

SET I:

- **Well-developed:** Working above the level for their age/grade placement in a specific academic area.

- **Developing as Expected:** Developing as expected in a given skill, concept, or behavioral area. This reflects progress that is appropriate for their age/grade placement.

- **Beginning to Develop:** Demonstrates interest in and participates to a limited degree in a specific activity. With time and experience, the child's level of understanding and concept development will reach an appropriate level.

- **Not Yet Apparent:** Has not yet shown any attempt to participate in a specific activity. This does not indicate failure, but it rather reflects differing rates of development.

SET II:

- **Consistently:** very good, always the same top quality

- **Usually:** good, often, most of the time

- **Occasionally:** fair but needs improvement, once in a while, now and then

- **Developing:** growth is being shown

- **Sometimes:** not often

- **Not Yet:** expectation has not been achieved

SET III:

- **CD—Consistently Demonstrating:** The student is independently applying and integrating skills that have been taught. On a regular basis he or she is showing continued understanding of the concept.

- **DV—Developing:** The student is in the process of learning and applying skills that have been taught. He or she is making steady growth toward understanding the concept.

- **NI—Needs Improvement:** The student is having difficulty in applying the skills that have been taught. He or she needs more practice to develop the understanding of the concept.

Now let's take a look at the descriptors and their definitions that we use throughout *this* book:

- **Developing:** A student at the *developing* stage is progressing toward competence in the subject area concerned.

> **WORTH NOTING:**
> Teachers do not always agree on the definitions for particular descriptors so, in effect, one teacher's C could be another's B. This isn't because teachers are confused about the definitions, but because some of them—particularly homeroom teachers in primary school—see students for longer periods of time than do others. Those teachers have the chance to perceive a child's progress not on a single project, test performance, or presentation, but against where he was before and what he is capable of and the shades of gray between these two poles. They see a glimpse of the whole person, from his irritating insistence of shouting out answers to his endearing readiness to nurse hurt butterflies. Descriptors are neat boxes and, though necessary, they don't always provide a perfect fit.

✔ **Capable:** A *capable* student demonstrates an adequate understanding of the subject area, processes the subject matter appropriately, and is competent in communicating the results of learning.

✔ **Proficient:** A *proficient* student demonstrates a good understanding of the subject concerned, processes the subject matter well, and communicates the results of learning clearly and effectively.

✔ **Excellent:** An *excellent* student demonstrates a thorough understanding of the subject concerned, processes the subject at a high level, and communicates the results of learning in a variety of clear, original, and thoughtful ways.

Finally, let's examine a table showing how the descriptors used in this book—*excellent, proficient, capable, developing,* and *needs improvement* (used rarely in this book)—line up with some of the other scales commonly used.

Descriptors Used in This Book	Other Common Descriptors as They Compare to Those in this Book					
EXCELLENT	Consistent	Always	Secure	Exceptional	Well-developed	Consistently demonstrating
PROFICIENT	Consistent	Almost always	Very good	Very competent	Well-developed	Usually demonstrating
CAPABLE	Usually	Often	Good	Competent	Developing as expected	Often
DEVELOPING	Beginning	Improving	Getting better	Satisfactory	Beginning to develop	Not always
NEEDS IMPROVEMENT*	Not observed	Not apparent	Needs time	Unsatisfactory	Occasionally	Sometimes

* *Used rarely in this book*

Report Card Narratives

Among different school systems' report cards, there is no standard amount of space allotted for the teacher's narrative comments. Sometimes the space allowed is wide open; other times it is quite limited. However, no matter what the allotted space, the teacher should take the time and effort to form cohesive paragraphs that build to a point or points. Too often, I have seen poorly constructed narratives. This can, unfortunately, affect the message that the teacher is trying to convey to the parents.

Following are some reminders that might help you in your own writing process:

✔ Be precise. Choose words carefully.

✔ Choosing the right word means you do not have to use too many of them. Brevity helps to make the writing concise and effective.

✔ Avoid jargon.

✔ Keep in mind your audience.

✔ Avoid repetition; the words *good, fine,* and *excellent* are acceptable if they are not overused—but they usually are. Find synonyms to avoid repetition.

✔ Increase the readability of the comment by:
- using sentences of varying length
- using a variety of sentence structures
- keeping the language simple
- using active verbs

WORTH NOTING:

To some extent, a teacher's personal philosophy of evaluation influences her perception of a student's performance. Simply put, the philosophy may be

- charting the point from where the student was to the point where the student now is.

- curriculum driven: based on how well the student does and how much learning the student shows on tests, assignments, and quizzes administered during the reporting period.

- comparative: charting the student's performance in relation to the other students in the class.

Depending on where a teacher stands on these three philosophies of evaluation, she may disagree with some of this book's categorizations. The comments in this book focus on curricular categories in which the child's performance is viewed in relation to his or her own potential, with the assumption that a child's effort and study habits are reflected in his or her work.

Within this framework, a student who made a big jump during a quarter in which enthusiasm for a topic encouraged him to read extensively, who was engaged in the tasks, and who produced superior work will be placed in the Excellent category. It is possible that in the next report card, he might find himself in the Capable category. Both evaluations reflect the student's performance in a given period against his potential and what he actually delivered.

However, a teacher with a different stance might, for example, believe that some comments in a chapter's Capable section belong to the Proficient section, or vice versa.

The chapters in the rest of the book offer hundreds of sample narratives. Before reading more about this topic, turn to one complete evaluation example (pages 13–16), a kind of student portrait.

Narrative Formats Teachers Frequently Use

In the best-case scenario, a student's performance drives the length of the narrative. Fortunately, there is no philosophy that dictates how many topics should be covered in a good report card narrative. Teachers subscribe to different ideas about this issue.

Following are the most popular positions among teachers:

1. Both the positive and the negative should be mentioned.

2. Omit areas in which the student has scored a good grade and let the mark speak for itself. Implicit here is the opinion that the teacher should get to the core—the area or areas in which the student has received poor grades.

3. In what may be called a "progressive" approach, the teacher continues with where she left off on the previous report card and tracks student performance between reporting periods.

While all of these formats are current and acceptable, none is exclusive. You can structure an informative and sensitive comment in a countless variety of ways. You may simply prefer one format over another, or may even change formats as you go along. In the end, you will likely find that you tend to vary formats for each student, and that what you choose is what is most effective for that particular situation.

A Detailed Look at One Student:
Elizabeth's Profile and Report Card

As she prepares to write a report card, the teacher attempts to take the three-dimensional reality of an individual student and translate this reality into the confines of a simple framework. Using information from tests, observations, anecdotal notes, assessment, and performance instruments, the teacher gleans student strengths, weaknesses, behavior, attitude, and study habits and knits together a profile that updates parents on their child's school performance.

This portrait includes collected raw data, the report card based upon the data, and the narrative that accompanies the report card. It should offer you a fully developed, walk-through illustration of the process of preparing and writing a report card and provide a kind of touchstone and context for the comments in the remainder of the book.

Elizabeth, Second Grader

The Teacher's Observations and Data About Elizabeth

LANGUAGE ARTS—READING

- Low reading level.
- IRI (1.1) first semester first grade reading level.
- Worked on word attack skills and predicting sentence patterns. Elizabeth does not absorb or apply these skills.
- Dolch sight word list: recognizes two-letter words; now beginning to recognize some three-letter words.

Strengths

- Strong oral skills.
- Listens well to stories.
- Responds appropriately.
- Participates in group discussions actively, and during these times it's easy to forget her lack of reading ability.
- Enjoys and listens attentively to books on tape and contributes with enthusiasm to the discussion that follows.

Weaknesses

At present reading level, is unable to:

- Read directions in math.
- Participate in choral reading of poems.
- Work on any research/writing project in language arts or social studies.

LANGUAGE ARTS—WRITING

- Shows a similar lack of skills in writing.
- Has to wait until the teacher can get to her to explain directions.
- Elaborates story ideas when brainstorming, but can't get going on writing.
- Encouraged to use inventive spelling, drawing, and labeling, but resists writing.

✔ Dictates story. Teacher often starts the dictation and then tells her to continue. When Elizabeth takes over, she adds a few short sentences and says she's finished.

MATH

Strength

✔ Does well in math; comfortable with straight basic operations and has sound understanding of math facts.

Weakness

✔ Word problems are difficult because she cannot read them, but she handles them when explained.

ACADEMIC CONCERNS

At Elizabeth's current rate of achievement (end of first semester, second grade), I fear that she may not be able to keep up with the class. She is one year behind in reading and writing, and this deficit is spilling over into math and science.

Elizabeth needs to take more responsibility, be more independent, and work harder toward achieving the goals of the second-grade curriculum.

Work habits/behavior/attitude

✔ Does not use her time well during reading and writing assignments.

✔ Doesn't seem to be trying enough.

✔ When Elizabeth focuses during direct instruction, she can succeed in figuring out math word problems.

✔ Often waits for information to be fed to her individually.

✔ Elizabeth makes friends easily enough, but she also loses them. Her overall attitude toward school is positive, though she is not strongly motivated with work requiring focus, paper and pencil, and some effort to read and write.

Notes on Meeting with Elizabeth's First-grade Teacher:

She said:

Elizabeth did not read at grade level when she left first grade. However, being able to read in first grade is not a requirement to move into second grade.

Elizabeth began to speak in sentences only in first grade. This was a big step that the first-grade teacher was nurturing, instead of loading Elizabeth with another task she was clearly finding difficult to do.

The Narrative

The narrative report on the report card read as follows:

Elizabeth's strong oral skills give her confidence to participate in story discussion, retell a story, and make predictions with ease. She needs to bring some of that enthusiasm to her writing and reading in order to achieve grade-level requirements.

(continued on page 16)

> Even as you start on a positive note you lay the groundwork for what is to come.

The Report Card, with Descriptors

Elizabeth's report card was filled in like this.

	1st	2nd	3rd	4th
LANGUAGE ARTS				
Reading Effort		NI		
Reading Achievement				
Comprehension		D		
Vocabulary		D		
Decoding		NI		
Writing Effort		NI		
Writing Achievement				
Expression of ideas		D		
Mechanics/Usage		NA		
Spelling		NA		
Handwriting		D		
Oral Skills		+		
Participation		+		
Listening Skills		+		
MATH				
Math Effort		✓+		
Math Achievement		✓		
Concept development		✓+		
Computes accurately		✓+		
Problem solving		✓+		
SCIENCE & SOCIAL STUDIES				
Effort				
Achievement				
Concept development		✓		
Class participation		✓+		
GENERAL BEHAVIOR				
Punctual and prepared		NI		
Works independently		NI		
Cooperates in groups		✓		
Respects others		✓		

Pupil: Elizabeth **Grade:** 2

Classroom Teacher: Mona Melwani

Explanation Key:

+ Excellent
✓+ Proficient
✓ Capable
D Developing
NI Needs Improvement
NA Not Applicable

Comments   2001–2002

The whole reading block indicates Elizabeth's needs to improve in this area.

Although mechanics and spelling are part of a second-grade program, Elizabeth is nowhere close to making sense of punctuation.. Marking it with NA lets you and the parent handle and focus on more important issues.

Elizabeth's good oral and listening skills are reflected here.

Because of Elizabeth's comfort with math and her quick understanding of it, her teacher believes that as soon as she begins to read, she will handle word problems as easily as she handles straight math problems. As it is, she grasps them quickly when the word problems are read to her, so she is considered proficient.

Elizabeth's need to work harder and be more responsible is shown here.

(Narrative report continued from page 14)

Currently, on the informal reading inventory (IRI), Elizabeth tested as an emergent reader. This is equivalent to a first-grade reading level. Consequently, Elizabeth has a hard time reading directions on assignments, and is unable to work on research and writing assignments in social studies and language arts. Elizabeth needs to work harder to raise her reading level.

> Support your contention with test results and how it is reflected in Elizabeth's work.

Our direct instruction in reading focuses continually on sound-symbol awareness (phonics), word attack skills, and prediction. I have worked one-on-one with Elizabeth to emphasize how this will help her decode. Nevertheless, she does not give her full attention to what best will help her, and she fails to apply these decoding skills.

> Show what is being done to help her and why the situation does not seem to be improving.

Elizabeth resists getting started on any kind of writing project. Her creative story ideas fascinate her peers when she brainstorms with them; however, she is not ready to write them yet. When she can be coaxed into trying, she writes a few short sentences but cannot fully develop her ideas.

> Prepare the parent for Elizabeth's lack of effort.

Elizabeth handles numbers comfortably and has a sound understanding of basic math operations. Unfortunately, her current reading level makes it difficult for her to handle word problems at this grade level.

> Indicate how Elizabeth's reading level is affecting areas she does well in.

Improving Elizabeth's reading level must be our central goal, because it will help her use her time well during reading and writing assignments and in other subject areas, as well.

Once you have decided upon a format and have assembled plenty of recorded information about a student's performance, all you need is to keep the language flowing lucidly in order to create a solid narrative.

An example of each of the three formats follows:

Format 1: Positive and Negative

This kind of narrative works well when a student is having trouble with specific areas within a subject. It allows the teacher to talk about the student's performance on the different topics studied during the period and to draw

> Begin with a general positive statement.

attention to areas the student is not handling well. It tells the parent that the child's ability is not in question but that time and practice will improve the child's understanding.

Eric is making steady progress on his math skills. Improved computation enhanced his speed work and he did particularly well on mental math quizzes.

> Single out a specific area within the subject that reflected this.

However, fractions and decimals still confuse him, and he has had to come in for some extra help.

The special homework he will be bringing home is intended to give him more practice with these problems. I feel certain that, with his persistence, Eric will soon be more secure in these areas of math.

> *Then focus on the specific area he needs help in.*

> *End on an encouraging note.*

Format 2: Poor Grade

For a student who is doing poorly, it is wise to spell out what exactly is being taught in class and what the student cannot seem to do. Information on how he or she is being helped in school and how the parents can assist is necessary. Although the emphasis in this format is on the difficulty that the student is having, it is thoughtful to highlight even a small area in which he or she is doing well.

Leah read twelve books independently this quarter. This steady improvement in reading is a result of her growing decoding skills.

> *An area she is growing in.*

A similar effort is required in writing, which continues to be difficult for her. In spite of the ideas generated in the classroom, Leah is at a loss when asked to choose a topic and does not know what to write about and how to start.

> *Area of concern. Leah's work behavior on writing assignments*

We have worked one-on-one to brainstorm ideas and identify resources she could use to develop her topic. However, Leah's writing assignments, both in language arts and in social studies, were poorly done.

> *The help that had been given*

Leah's lack of effort and her unwillingness to use the help provided concerns me. As the year progresses, we expect to investigate other genres in literature and to write more. In social studies, our research topics and research reports will require skills that Leah should have acquired by now.

> *She is behind in these skills and may have difficulty with the challenges ahead.*

Leah needs to be encouraged to view writing as an enjoyable activity. Perhaps a family writing activity (like the one enclosed) would help her to do so.

> *Involve parents to support Leah and the teacher.*

Format 3: The Progressive Comment

This structure works especially well in the case of a student who received a poor grade in the previous report. The teacher needs to follow through on the problem areas by directly addressing those particular work and academic behaviors.

> *Adam's problem and progress is implied in the first sentence with precise use of the word notable.*

Notable strides in spelling and math describe Adam's progress this quarter.

Adam's spelling scores have gone up and he is now approaching more challenging words. In math, Adam sailed through decimals and percents comfortably.

> *Specific examples are provided.*

During this period, Adam has come in every Monday ready with his weekly poem, which he recites in class without embarrassment. This is a positive development, and your support has been helpful in achieving this.

> *A particular concern in which the parent was involved is handled.*

Report Cards and the Parent-Teacher Relationship

Because parents and teachers have such a far-reaching effect on the life of a child, the dynamics of the teacher-parent relationship deserve attention. Communication is the cornerstone of this relationship; sincerity is its pillar. Teachers who observe and engage with their students every day—and, in some cases, all day—develop almost a sixth sense about each student. This becomes evident to parents in the constructive and caring way teachers approach their children's problems, and in the teacher's willingness to listen, to share, and to partner with parents. For this reason, there is no need for—or room for—a casual approach when talking or writing to parents about their child.

Educating Parents

The school has the specific responsibility of helping parents understand the growth and development of their child. Therefore, it is important that parents are educated about the philosophy on which the school's report card is based. For example, the currently popular developmental continuum favors tracking a student's progress from where he or she was upon entering the class to how he or she is moving along. This can be disconcerting for parents who seek in a report card information about their child's performance in relation to the other students in class, and not about the progress he has made. Parents need to understand not only the nature of the developmental report card, but also the manner in which the report card reflects the child's development.

Some Delicate Situations

No matter which culture you are operating within, bad news requires the utmost care. The following scenarios apply to report card narratives as well as parent conferences in such special circumstances.

Scenario 1: Motivation and Performance Concerns

Informing parents of their child's poor performance and improper classroom behavior is an unpleasant task, hence the need for careful planning before such a conference. Sara is one such case.

Sara indicates by her classroom manner, and by her social interaction in and out of the classroom, that she is intelligent and understands classroom expectations but is not interested in achieving them. She wiles away her time, starts work late and then hurries towards the end, submitting careless and unfinished work. The teacher, Ms. K., has called for a parent conference.

Ms. K. starts by pointing out Sara's strengths and then focuses on her weaknesses. A negative statement about Sara's work or behavior is further amplified by samples of student work. Neither in tone nor manner does the presentation of the sample convey, "Look, here's proof," but rather, "This is what I mean." Ms. K. follows the presentation of the samples by offering supportive ways to help the student.

While Mrs. K. gives details about Sara's lack of responsibility, she also suggests how Sara could be helped to be more responsible. Initially, the parent may not be able to think of a single or definite way to do this, especially if the news is a surprise. This uncertainty, along with any negative feelings, must be allayed to make parents effective partners in this process.

One way to facilitate parents' input is to help them discover what they already know about their child. After all, some of the behaviors that teachers report are those the parents see at home as well—and are trying to handle themselves. The parents' contribution at this point will let the teacher know:

- What has been tried
- What has worked and what hasn't
- What other options might be tried

Once this list has been compiled, it may be clear that some behaviors are never seen at home but appear only in the classroom. These behaviors give a teacher the most food for thought.

Sometimes the teacher may ask questions to elicit parent input if the parents are reticent or unable initially to say much. In such an instance, Ms. K. might ask these questions about Sara's behavior at home:

- What are some things Sara does for herself at home?
- What are some chores Sara is responsible for?
- How well does she do those chores?
- How can we make sure Sara completes her chores to satisfaction?
- How should we reinforce work done on time and well?

The data gathered assists in creating a plan for Sara.

Scenario 2: Significant Problems

In this scenario, the student's performance or behavior seriously affects his or her progress. Because negative feedback distresses parents, teachers tend to avoid it and may merely drop hints instead. However, if a student's problematic work, behavior, or attitude needs to be reported, it's best to do it directly and to do it early. Consider the case of Jack.

Jack's academic performance is way too low, and his attitude and behavior are major hindrances to his progress. The teacher, Mrs. T., knows the parents shouldn't have to hear this first from a report card, especially since Jack's lack of academic focus is evident long before the close of the reporting period. A parent conference is in order.

Parents have many reactions to bad news; they can become argumentative, grow quiet, sit in shocked silence, or blame the teacher. It is easy for parents to feel defensive about their children. Basically, they are overwhelmed and the truth is that it hurts to hear your child is doing poorly. The teacher needs to be sympathetic and keep the doors to communication open.

Mrs. T. knows this and works with Jack's parents during the conference, not against them. After conveying her concerns and alerting the parents to Jack's problems, she then sets up a plan with the parents' input (just as Ms. K. did in Sara's case above). A schedule for following up on the plan weekly or daily is established, and the plan is signed by the parents and the teacher. The success of this partnership will depend on how closely the follow-up is maintained.

Scenario 3: The Parent Blind Spot

In this situation, the teacher clearly and sympathetically describes the student's problem to the parents, but the parents can't see what the problem is and why the teacher is making such a big deal about it.

The teacher's view is:

"Your child's behavior is unacceptable in school; it is affecting his education and that of the others in the classroom as well. Here are some rules we try to follow in class so that we can work well together and move on with our academics. However, Bill…"

The parents' view is:

"I don't see the problem. He's only ten years old, he's a kid, it's normal for his age. I have four kids, they've all been like this, they're growing up just fine."

This is a delicate situation, because there is so little support from the parents. Yet the teacher needs to keep trying, because this child needs her help the most. Consider the case of Bill:

Bill, a fourth grader, is squirmy and wiggly with a short attention span. He is frequently in play mode, carrying mini cars and computer games in his pocket. At any time in the middle of a lesson or quiet story time, he thinks nothing of pulling them out and playing with them. When they are confiscated, he finds some other way to play, like by drumming his fingers on the desk. He always manages to divert the attention of the other students as well.

He calls out without waiting his turn, is frequently noisy, and does not seem to mind staying in during recess to finish up his work.

Three possible reasons for Bill's behavior are:

- ✔ He wants attention.
- ✔ He is having a hard time coping with the work and is using this behavior to cover that up.
- ✔ He is angry, wants to strike back, and chooses confrontation.

There are also other less likely but legitimate possibilities. For instance, Bill might be young for the class, or he might be the right age but developmentally immature.

Sending the report card home without giving the parent any prior notice of Bill's behavior is unreasonable. In fact, Bill's teacher has spoken on the phone to the parents and held a conference as soon as the situation became apparent. During those earlier conversations, the parents exposed their blind spot to the teacher. Knowing this situation was quite complex, the teacher also called on the support of the school counselor to observe Bill and to ask for some ways to handle the situation.

Bill's teacher is now at this point:

- ✔ The parents are not going to be surprised at the report card.
- ✔ The teacher has tried to hold Bill to task with the counselor's support.

Here is the narrative on Bill's report card:

Bill is having a hard time keeping up with class work. In the last two weeks, he has stayed in four times during recess to complete his assignments. During these time-outs, it is surprising how well he can do when he puts his mind to it.

Yet, Bill does not seem as interested in attending to instructions given in class or working on his tasks. He is frequently off task and distracting to other students as well.

I drew your attention to this problem at our meeting on the 29th of September, and I regret to report that Bill's behavior has not improved since then. We need to discuss this further.

I would like to have a conference with you next week to discuss how we can help Bill. Please let me know a day that will be convenient for you.

In preparation for this conference the teacher should:

- ✔ Keep ready the assignments Bill did well during recess, along with the samples of poor work done in class when he was not attentive.
- ✔ Maintain a running record of what the teacher has tried with the counselor's help.
- ✔ Schedule the counselor to be present at the upcoming conference.
- ✔ Perhaps consider taking pictures of Bill (if school policy permits) involved in different activities at various times of the day. The pictures will contrast Bill's behavior against that of the other students in the class and may prove one concrete way that the parents can recognize the problem.

The teacher should recognize, even as she arms herself with the above preparations, that the parents probably need help as well. Her approach should therefore be as sensitive and empathetic as possible.

Scenario 4: The Generation Gap

The newer methods of assessment and evaluation arising from advances in education research and theory, and the vast, continually-evolving vocabulary in this field can be mind-boggling. Not surprisingly, parents cannot relate their own experiences to the new knowledge. It is difficult for them to help their children with homework or comprehend the teacher if they don't understand what the language means.

Sometimes all the education that may be required is to explain what the new words mean in terms of old, familiar words. However, some of the newer methods are far too different to draw a comparison between old and new. Recognizing this, some schools do educate parents in the new curricula and programs the school is adopting. Further, the publishers of many new textbook programs are well aware of the difference between the old and new ways, and offer newsletters to go home with each new unit.

Nonetheless, there remain some parents who have no idea about these new approaches and programs. How does one explain to these parents that their child is having a problem?

First, it is essential to make an effort to explain the following:

- What the goal of a subject and specific unit of study is.
- How the teacher plans to achieve that goal (with readings, activities, projects, etc.).
- What the students have to do to achieve the goal.

With a prelude like this, it should not be difficult to give parents a fair idea of how their child is doing. Consider the case of Sophia.

Our unit on graphs this quarter aimed at collecting information and classifying it appropriately. Sophia chose to discover which ice cream flavors were popular in third grade.

> *The project and its purpose simply told.*

After polling the students, her next step was to graph the numbers on a bar chart. Finally, she had to understand what the graph meant by explaining which flavors she would stock if she had an ice cream stall.

> *The steps she had to follow.*

Sophia transferred numbers from the ice cream survey to the graph accurately. She also interpreted the information correctly to conclude that she would stock up on chocolate ice cream. Please have a look at her graph when she brings it home at the end of this week.

> *What she did correctly, plus an opportunity for a parent to see and hear what Sophia learned.*

The Good News Narrative

We now turn to another kind of scenario. Here the students are doing consistently well in all areas. How does one comment on this without simply repeating what was already said in the previous quarters?

Scenario 5: When the News Is Good

First, no matter how regularly and steadily the student is moving along, academic progress needs to be described. Even though the message may be the same, it is so important that it bears repeating. Second, there is always some growth between reporting periods to report—in both academic as well as in social-emotional behaviors and work habits.

Observation notes will indicate specific details about the student's participation in cooperative groups, maturing behaviors during shared reading and listening, changes in the student's response to stories, progress with oral and written reports, and so on. These developments need to be reported. Parents with children who are conscientious and hardworking deserve to know this.

Finally, list some of the important skills you focused on in the units you taught during this period and then explicitly point out how well the student achieved them.

Reporting student work to parents requires communication on an ongoing basis to help build an open, mutually supportive relationship. This relationship impacts the student's performance, whether the student is having problems or experiencing great success in school.

CHAPTER 2

Language Arts

LANGUAGE ARTS INCLUDES THE four integrated areas of reading, writing, speaking, and listening. Every language arts program includes a scope and sequence as well as a list of skills to be met under each of the four areas. Language arts is central to academic success and, thus, positive qualities developed here can be transferred to other subjects. The self-esteem and confidence that students build here are attitudes they will carry to science, social studies, and math.

The narrative comments in this chapter deal with all four language arts areas—reading, writing, speaking, and listening—although, admittedly, there is a leaning toward writing and reading. Because of the current emphasis on writing and the writing process in particular, many of the comments here include references to creative work, punctuation, and editing skills.

In this chapter, as with others, you will undoubtedly make best use of the comments presented if you modify them by adding what is relevant to your own particular classroom.

Before the four sets of comments are presented, we'll take a look at a sample report card and narrative, with the language arts area highlighted. Here we look at the evaluation of Chi Young, who has achieved a rating of Excellent.

A Detailed Look at the Language Arts Evaluation of an Excellent Student: *Chi Young, Fifth Grader*

Writing narratives for the outstanding student appears the easiest report card to write, and it is. Yet such students (and their parents) are concerned about their report cards as much as anyone. They are usually interested in specific details—details these students probably pore over to find out how to keep doing their best. They deserve to know that their extra effort showed, was noticed, and that it enhanced their work. This is the best reinforcement for the Excellent student. Chi Young falls into this category.

The Report Card, with Descriptors

Chi Young's report card was filled in like this.

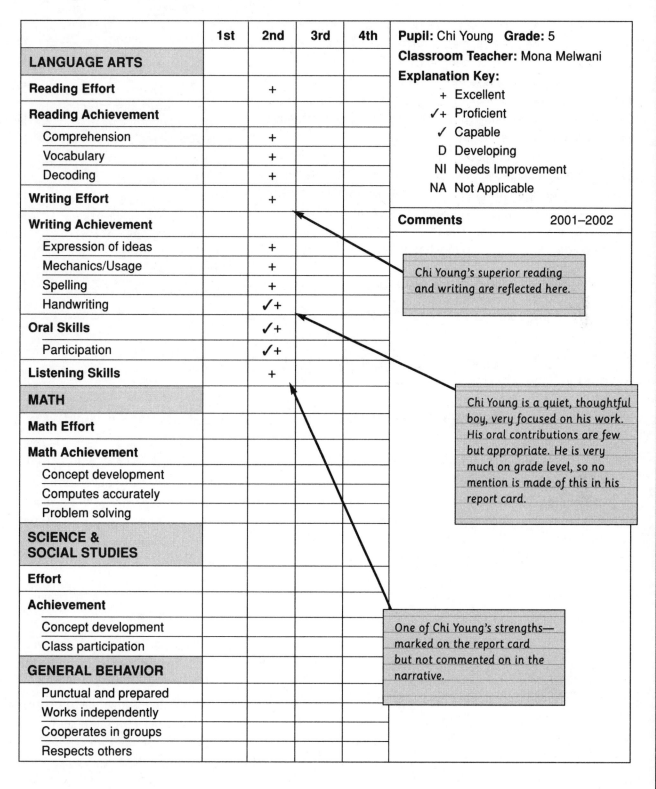

	1st	2nd	3rd	4th
LANGUAGE ARTS				
Reading Effort		+		
Reading Achievement				
Comprehension		+		
Vocabulary		+		
Decoding		+		
Writing Effort		+		
Writing Achievement				
Expression of ideas		+		
Mechanics/Usage		+		
Spelling		+		
Handwriting		✓+		
Oral Skills		✓+		
Participation		✓+		
Listening Skills		+		
MATH				
Math Effort				
Math Achievement				
Concept development				
Computes accurately				
Problem solving				
SCIENCE & SOCIAL STUDIES				
Effort				
Achievement				
Concept development				
Class participation				
GENERAL BEHAVIOR				
Punctual and prepared				
Works independently				
Cooperates in groups				
Respects others				

Pupil: Chi Young **Grade:** 5

Classroom Teacher: Mona Melwani

Explanation Key:
+ Excellent
✓+ Proficient
✓ Capable
D Developing
NI Needs Improvement
NA Not Applicable

Comments   2001–2002

Chi Young's superior reading and writing are reflected here.

Chi Young is a quiet, thoughtful boy, very focused on his work. His oral contributions are few but appropriate. He is very much on grade level, so no mention is made of this in his report card.

One of Chi Young's strengths—marked on the report card but not commented on in the narrative.

The Narrative

The narrative on his report card says it all:

Chi Young enjoys school and has enthusiasm for everything we do.

His love of books contributes to the high level of reading comprehension he has achieved. Chi Young tested at sixth-grade level on the reading assessment test.

Ideas crowd Chi Young's head when we get into creative writing, and he does have trouble organizing his stories. Nevertheless, he persists in completing his task, going through two or three drafts until he gets it just right.

Our writing assignment this quarter was integrated with the Social Studies unit on the Amazon Rain Forest. The assignment called for creating an adventure set in the rain forest with details that demonstrate an understanding of this unique habitat and its animals. Chi Young's story, "The Python and the Piranha," contained details and description that amply fulfilled these requirements.

Chi Young's consistent effort is commendable.

> The superlatives used for Chi Young's reading are supported by the reading assessment. His writing effort and persistence include the organizing and proofreading skills he is gaining.

> The assignment objective defines curricular goals and serves to inform parents what teachers mean by integration.

> A specific example backs up the progress noticed. The narrative ends with a commendation.

Sample Narratives for Developing Students

Progressive Comment

1. John participated in class discussions this quarter and was also willing to do his share of tasks in the project on rocks. This is a pleasing development.

He appears more willing to cooperate and work together with his peers. This has helped him to make some friends, so that he can now find a partner for shared reading time and when we pair off for math games.

Overall, John's attitude and attention have improved, and it shows in all areas of his work.

✓ ✓ ✓ ✓

Positive and Negative

2. Improved reading comprehension and a growing vocabulary are noteworthy gains Vinisha made this semester. If she keeps up her hard work, she will meet the reading requirements of fourth grade.

In writing, Vinisha is slowly developing skills that allow her to express herself easily. At this time, she struggles to construct complete sentences and is somewhat frustrated with her inability to convey her ideas.

Vinisha would benefit from reading this summer. She could also keep a journal.

✓ ✓ ✓ ✓

Just the Right Words: 201 Report Card Comments • Scholastic Teaching Resources

3. David is working hard on acquiring English. His limited vocabulary makes it difficult for him to convey his ideas either orally or in writing.

Our language lessons at this time focus on sentence structure and verb tense. Our vocabulary lessons are ongoing. In the weeks to come, David will have opportunities to practice and develop skills which will help him tackle writing tasks at the fifth-grade level.

Currently, David corrects capitalization and spelling errors in assigned sentences, but is unable to integrate these rules in his independent writing tasks.

A valuable goal for David next quarter is to take more time to read over his work and edit it with care.

✓ ✓ ✓ ✓ ✓

ESL

4. Benjamin strives hard to complete his assignments, although they are difficult and frustrating for him. Just one quarter of exposure to the English language is too short of a period to acquire fluency and comprehension at the third-grade level. Under these circumstances, Benjamin's effort is commendable.

Benjamin's reading responses—expressed in his beautiful artwork—successfully communicate his understanding of what he has read and what he feels about the story.

Benjamin should use his summer constructively with lots of reading and some journal writing. This would help him capitalize on his gains in language this semester.

✓ ✓ ✓ ✓ ✓

ESL

5. A good listener, Jorie eagerly attempts assignments even though she can't always understand them. She is also very shy and hesitates to ask for help. As she gains more language, I hope she will feel more comfortable to ask for help. In the meantime, she observes others and follows directions as best she can.

Jorie has acquired many friends in class through her positive attitude and cheerful manner.

✓ ✓ ✓ ✓ ✓

ESL

6. Kate's reading skills have improved considerably this year. She now decodes faster using both visual and context clues to make sense.

Writing is still difficult for Kate. Often she does not know what to write about and has a hard time getting started. At other times she starts on a topic and runs out of things to say after a few sentences.

We have worked together to brainstorm ideas and have singled out resources she could use to develop her topic. Although she is getting better, Kate needs to put more effort into developing her ideas for writing.

✓ ✓ ✓ ✓ ✓

Point to what the student is doing well. Highlight the area she needs to work on.

Positive and Negative

7. Steady progress in reading and writing characterize Sophie's performance this quarter. Sophie is now reading at grade level. She has graduated to books which have a lot more words than pictures in them.

During buddy reading, Sophie shares her favorite books in an expressive voice and with growing fluency.

Her confidence is showing in other ways as well; she handles class tasks independently and takes responsible citizenship roles in the classroom.

Sophie worked hard this quarter and should keep up the good work by continuing to read books she enjoys.

✓ ✓ ✓ ✓ ✓

8. Serena has made satisfactory progress this quarter.

In language arts, she kept pace with her classroom assignments and also with her homework reading. The support you have given her has done much to help Serena see the importance of putting her best effort in her work.

Serena's improved reading comprehension is obvious in the insights and opinions she shares about what she has read. Additionally, she can now retell the main points of a story in sequence.

This has been a productive quarter for Serena.

✓ ✓ ✓ ✓ ✓

make(ing) satisfactory progress
Synonyms:
improving
becoming better
growing
advancing
moving forward
moving ahead
progressing
achieving a higher level

9. Lindsay has made progress in writing this quarter. She understands word order and can make simple sentences. These are big steps in the writing process—steps which Lindsay needs to maintain.

At this time, her effort is not consistent; the quality of her work drops noticeably when she is not concentrating.

In reading, we are learning strategies to figure out the meaning of new words (context clues) and to decode unfamiliar ones. These are helpful tools that Lindsay should practice while reading at home.

Perhaps if she has the opportunity to read aloud to an adult, this practice will be more enjoyable for her. I know she responds well to encouragement.

✓ ✓ ✓ ✓ ✓

This active student cannot sit still. He gets up often from his seat to look for a book or sharpen his pencil—often in the middle of instruction. Because he is not paying attention, he often does not know the directions for an assignment. As a result, his work is frequently incomplete, hurriedly done, and of poor quality.

10. Although Ben is bright and energetic and keeps busy all the time, it is unfortunate that he is usually not busy with academic tasks. He is often out of his seat and off task. It is not surprising that many of his assignments are now overdue. Further, those that he has submitted are of poor quality, indicating Ben's lack of interest in class work.

To help Ben stay on task, I gave him an assignment book intended to make it easier for him to keep track of work to be completed and submitted. For now, it is helping him to bring his homework in more regularly.

I pointed out these concerns to you at our conference last month, and would like to reiterate that Ben needs to become more serious about and give his full attention to his school work. I am eager to see him start showing this.

✓ ✓ ✓ ✓ ✓

11. Improved reading has enabled Eva to enjoy books a lot more. The numerous books she has checked out this quarter are evidence of her enthusiasm. Books on tape continue to be Eva's favorites.

Eva is still shy. She seldom asks questions or volunteers to answer in class. I am also concerned that she is not making friends.

✓ ✓ ✓ ✓ ✓

12. Shu Li Yen's reading advanced significantly in the last three weeks of this quarter. Fascinated by the solar system, his curiosity took him to the reference section of the library. He has since checked out chapter books on science fiction topics and is rapidly reading through them.

Unfortunately, Shu Li Yen is not very fond of writing. Even a research report seems like too much effort for him. He is now working with a "report organizer" to help him build each part of his report. He then has to move on to connecting the paragraphs to complete the report.

We continue to work on editing and revising skills in our writing lessons, and Shu Li Yen will need to learn and practice these skills.

✓ ✓ ✓ ✓ ✓

> Positive and Negative

13 Daniel is slowly developing as a reader. He now demonstrates one-to-one correspondence and recognizes that words are separated by spaces.

In writing, he takes great care in forming his letters and can recognize most of them. The concept of inventive spelling—putting together the appropriate letters to make the sounds of the words he wants to write—is still not clear to him.

Although Daniel requires a lot of support at this time, he is willing to work hard and he gives each task his best effort.

✓ ✓ ✓ ✓ ✓

> Highlight what the student is doing well.

14. Evan has a charming way of expressing himself in his writing. He loves to tell a story, adding drama and action in his dialogue.

On the other hand, Evan is not as enthusiastic about editing and proofreading. He needs a lot of encouragement to work on these skills, and is able to create a satisfactory final product only after a great deal of prodding.

Evan wrote two books this quarter, "My Favorite Computer Game" and "The Monarch Butterfly," and both were completed with beautiful illustrations.

✓ ✓ ✓ ✓ ✓

15. Mark's progress this year has been unpredictable. There are times when he works, and there are times when he does not seem motivated to work at all. On these latter occasions, his work leaves much to be desired.

His book talk on *The Diary of Anne Frank* was well prepared and presented. In contrast, his report on *The Hunchback of Notre Dame* was four sentences long and so did not contain the essential ingredients of a report.

Some situations demand coming to the point right away. In such instances, it is important to conclude with a goal the student can point toward.

Although Mark's reading performance is on grade level, I believe he is capable of achieving more. I have encouraged him to attempt chapter books or start reading a series by an author he likes; however, he doesn't seem willing to extend himself.

✓ ✓ ✓ ✓

Sample Narratives for Capable Students

1. Jin enjoys writing and has taken his first steps in developing his own stories. The large body of high-frequency words he has acquired allows him to write many sentences.

ESL

English grammar, however, is still new to Jin. Although he understands it, he has not yet been able to integrate it into his own writing. Jin needs time and more practice to do so. As he continues to listen to and read stories, these skills will grow.

Jin is a hardworking student. He uses the dictionary and refers to his word bank often.

✓ ✓ ✓ ✓

Name specific skills and processes the student is achieving.

2. Kirstin improved her reading comprehension this year and pursued this goal steadily throughout the year. As she grew more confident, she began to readily participate in class activities.

Kirstin was actively engaged in the reading research project on autobiography. She selected books to read independently and was able to recall facts from informational texts.

confident
Synonyms:
 comfortable
 competent
 skillful
 secure

Hard work and dedication contributed to the leap Kirstin has made in reading this year.

✓ ✓ ✓ ✓

3. Vadim is making satisfactory progress in English.

He is always willing to give his input during class meetings; in fact, he occasionally has to be asked to stop and allow others to have a say.

When Vadim does share, he needs to speak up and speak clearly so that he can be better heard and understood.

Writing is not always easy for beginning learners of English. At this time, Vadim's writing generally contains numerous run-on sentences and fragments, which he will learn to identify as his experience with English grows.

✓ ✓ ✓ ✓

Positive and Negative

4. Substantial gains in vocabulary and reading summarize Josh's progress this year. His focus on meeting the demands of our challenging fifth-grade literature was well rewarded.

It would have been splendid if he had given as much attention to acquiring good listening habits. As you know, Josh always needs directions repeated to him because he tends to tune out when instructions are being given. As a result, his listening and speaking vocabulary is not as strong as it could be. He has a difficult time retelling a story in sequence.

I have encouraged Josh to listen to books on tape and will be sending a book and tape home every week to help him practice. He is also working in the classroom on computer software that requires him to listen and respond.

Start on what the student is doing well, then point to an area of weakness on which he needs to work.

✓✓✓✓

5. As Monique learns and uses new strategies for approaching unfamiliar words, her reading is gaining fluency.

During our study of early American colonization, Monique's class presentation indicated a sound understanding of informational text. Our literature studies incorporated a lot of non-fictional reading as well, and Monique seemed to enjoy these books.

Organized and attentive, Monique is a responsible student.

✓✓✓✓

6. Rainer's writing skills continue to develop steadily. This quarter we learned to extend our writing ideas using description and details. Rainer's wonderful imagination enabled him to use these skills to build his story, "The Witch's Hat."

The next step in our writing program is to learn to use plot and setting to structure an adventure story. I feel confident that Rainer will continue to give his best effort.

✓✓✓✓

7. Lavina is excited about reading and has learned to figure out all the signs in the classroom. She selects simple books to read as a free activity.

Along with her reading, Lavina's writing is also developing. She matches letter sounds to words correctly and uses inventive spelling to write. Bursting with ideas, Lavina is eager to share her stories.

Lavina is enjoying her thrilling new achievements, and should be given every encouragement to keep at it.

✓✓✓✓

8. Jesse enjoys reading and sharing what he has read with the class. During the last few weeks, he worked on reading louder so he could be heard. In the process, he improved his diction (pronunciation). The result is that he has now acquired a pleasing fluency as well as a clear reading voice. He frequently volunteers to read aloud in class.

As class helper of the day two weeks ago, Jesse entertained the students with a dramatized performance of *The Little Red Hen*.

Jesse is a pleasure to have in class.

✓✓✓✓

9. Jordan showed marked improvement in writing and reading this quarter.

In reading, he moved to a higher level this semester, testing well on comprehension and decoding. He has reason to be proud of his achievement, as he is now on grade level.

Jordan's budding writing skills are evident in the longer, more complex sentences he is writing, particularly when he works on book reports. Furthermore, he pays close attention to our mini-lessons on punctuation and word order. This has helped to making his writing flow more smoothly.

Jordan can be relied on to follow class rules. He also puts his best effort into his work.

Sample Narratives for Proficient Students

1. A keen reader and writer, Claire made significant gains in both reading and writing.

You are already aware of Claire's love of reading, which now encompasses a variety of genres.

This quarter, her writing was marked by both the use of new vocabulary that she is incorporating and the steady sharpening of her proofreading skills. Her recent persuasion piece, "Holland: Land of Windmills and Tulips," showed progress in vocabulary, organization, and grammar.

A conscientious student, Claire puts excellent thought and effort into each assignment.

✓ ✓ ✓ ✓

2. Peter is making fine progress in his reading performance this quarter. His sight vocabulary improved and he is now working on the two hundred most common sight words (on the Dolch list that we use as our standard). This has helped him advance from reading word by word to reading complete sentences.

Peter has integrated two valuable reading strategies: he pauses to decode multi-syllabic words, and he uses context to identify difficult vocabulary.

Peter's commendable performance must be encouraged. His goal for the next quarter is to complete his reading log assignments so that he remains engaged in reading comprehension.

✓ ✓ ✓ ✓

3. Justine has consolidated the gains she made in reading the last quarter. Her sight vocabulary has expanded, as has her understanding of text. The result is that Justine is reading fluently and with fine expression. Her oral presentations are a pleasure to listen to.

Justine is an attentive student and often completes tasks before the allotted time given.

✓ ✓ ✓ ✓

4. Anthony expresses himself admirably orally and in his writing.

Using his growing bank of known words, he is becoming more and more articulate.

The insightful thoughts that Anthony shares reflect the knowledge he is gaining from his vast reading.

A good listener, Anthony is able to grasp concepts and ask good questions.

He now needs to direct his attention to editing and revising his work, because he often overlooks errors such as indenting paragraphs and using quotation marks.

Anthony thinks critically about what he has read. He makes thoughtful comments during class discussions.

✓ ✓ ✓ ✓

5. Julie works eagerly and diligently on all language assignments. Her creativity is evident in the interesting details and intriguing dialog she includes in her stories.

Two books Julie completed this quarter hold an enviable place in our class library: "Tall, Tall Girl" and "If the Hare Had Won the Race." These stories give evidence of Julie's ability to develop her ideas with logical sequence and a knowledge of story elements.

Julie is maturing into a sensitive writer and should be encouraged to keep up the good work.

✓ ✓ ✓ ✓

The Good News Narrative

6. Deidre has fit in with her new school and classmates with ease. She has made friends and does not lack partners during shared reading times.

Deidre is not shy about asking questions, and the discussions springing from those questions help her to clarify her own thinking. She makes perceptive contributions in group discussions.

In writing, Deidre can expand on the main idea, developing it by adding description and details.

At this time, she is learning to organize her ideas. Her recent pieces have been better planned than earlier ones.

Deidre is a caring and cooperative student.

✓ ✓ ✓ ✓

7. Andrew is maturing into a wonderful reader and writer.

His best work this quarter was the culminating activity on our folklore unit. After we had read a variety of myths and fairy tales and reflected on their characteristics, Andrew submitted his own fairy tale. It was descriptive, imaginative, and humorous. "The Chair That Wouldn't Seat" did a beautiful job illustrating his understanding of this genre.

Well done, Andrew!

✓ ✓ ✓ ✓

The Good News Narrative

ESL

8. Jean is eager to acquire English fast. Our daily drills in grammar and writing are helping her to practice strong English skills. We are also working on writing skills. She can now write short, complete sentences with correct grammar. In the coming months, we will build on this foundation so Jean will learn to develop new ideas and write more about them.

There are many fourth-grade assignments requiring a higher level of English than what Jean is capable of, and she cannot do these yet. This is understandable for a student new to English; however, Jean needs to accept that she is not ready yet to do all of the fourth-grade work. Her enthusiasm and eagerness to do all of the assignments frustrates her.

✓ ✓ ✓ ✓ ✓

9. Gerard's eagerness to learn and his positive attitude have contributed to the great strides he has made in English since he joined our class in the second semester.

His confidence is evident when he asks questions and volunteers to participate in the activities even with his limited English.

Socially, Gerard's fine sense of humor and his sharing attitude have made him many friends. This willingness to interact has helped both his confidence and his vocabulary.

Gerard continues to work on his writing skills. His basic sentence structure is at a beginning level at this time. However, this is a significant achievement, since he has been exposed to English for just two months.

His enthusiasm for learning makes Gerard a pleasure to have in class.

✓ ✓ ✓ ✓ ✓

10. Emma is a good team worker. She enjoys group projects and makes a real effort to bring the group together to share in the work. Her leadership skills are well developed.

Writing continues to be Emma's favorite subject. She weaves her imagination and creative ideas into interesting, fantastic pieces for which she has many listeners in class.

Emma is learning how to order her material in a readable sequence and experimenting with connecting ideas and using paragraphs appropriately.

Attention to punctuation is a good goal for Emma for the next quarter.

✓ ✓ ✓ ✓ ✓

ESL

11. Inez works wholeheartedly on her language assignments. Eager to acquire English fast, she attempts every task assigned, many of which are actually quite difficult for her. However, she listens carefully and tries to follow directions by observing others.

Inez now reads at a level below grade level, but I am confident that with the determination she is currently showing, she will achieve the required standard by the end of the year.

✓ ✓ ✓ ✓

12. Sarah is an enthusiastic reader and writer. She works diligently and responsibly.

Her creative writing overflows with interesting details and intriguing dialogue. Sarah wrote two books this quarter: "What Katy Didn't Do," a piece of fiction, and "The Howler Monkey," which was based on research she did. These works highlight how Sarah is learning to develop writing for different purposes.

Sarah is a pleasure to have in class; she is well-mannered and considerate toward her classmates.

✓ ✓ ✓ ✓

13. Jada is an avid reader. She comes to fifth grade prepared with skills that will help her meet the challenges of our science and literature program.

Jada is also a good listener. She doesn't hesitate to ask questions, and her insightful contributions demonstrate that she is quite reflective as well.

In writing, Jada has learned to combine sentences effectively and is able to write complex sentences with the use of a comma.

Jada is a conscientious student who is meticulous about working carefully and submitting her work on time.

✓ ✓ ✓ ✓

It is particularly important to report progress in English for students for whom English is a second language.

ESL

14. Simone has developed a large body of common words for reading and writing. Along with this, she has become increasingly aware of new vocabulary. Both of these developments were evident in her recent piece, "My Tokyo." Her piece called "Egyptian Mummies" was carefully researched. She worked through three drafts, editing and proofreading her work as she went along. The final version she submitted was a well-balanced piece that was both interesting and informative.

Simone shows enthusiasm for learning and is willing to extend herself.

✓ ✓ ✓ ✓

15. Tina is maturing into an elegant and creative writer. She has many ideas, and she expands and organizes them well.

This quarter we learned how to combine sentences and use modifiers to extend sentences. Tina applies these skills to add interesting details to her stories.

Now that her academic progress and seat work are progressing satisfactorily, I would like to see Tina participate more in group and shared projects. She needs to come out of her shell, speak up, and share her ideas during class discussions.

Tina's enjoyment of reading has led her to read high-level chapter books; however, I would like her to practice reading aloud, preferably to an adult, so that she can get used to speaking in a louder, clearer voice. This is a good skill to have when making presentations as well.

✓ ✓ ✓ ✓

Tina, a smart student, is shy and quiet. She is passive and does not participate in whole-group discussion or share and contribute in group projects. She finds it hard to find a partner during shared reading time. This has not helped her to make friends. Her reading aloud is poor, as her voice is soft and the class only hears a mumble. To get her parents involved, her teacher calls for their help in listening to her read.

Progressive
Comment

16. Thomas's reading is moving ahead satisfactorily.

During this quarter, he has acquired helpful reading strategies, which enable him to use his knowledge of language to predict words in the text. His facility to use context to identify difficult vocabulary is helping him move toward becoming an excellent reader.

The next goal for Thomas is to turn his attention to listening carefully to instruction. He needs to concentrate on what is being said so that he is able to follow concepts and directions independently.

Thomas should continue to get the support in reading and writing that you are giving him.

✓ ✓ ✓ ✓ ✓

Sample Narratives for Excellent Students

Highlight area of strength.

1. Maya expresses herself admirably both orally and in her writing. Her written expression reflects the fluency and imagination of one who reads widely and well.

A vast vocabulary and strong comprehension aid Maya in thinking critically about what she has read. She communicates her views with insight and clarity.

Maya's proofreading skills are so well integrated that she has served as a peer proofreader, helping other students with punctuation and spelling.

A conscientious student, Maya performs well in everything she undertakes.

✓ ✓ ✓ ✓ ✓

While spotlighting this student's proficiency in one subject, the teacher keeps parents informed about other skills he will be learning.

2. A talented writer, Shiva uses imagination and vivid description to draw effective word pictures. Incorporating humor and dialogue, Shiva varies sentence structure to make his writing interesting to the reader. He understands English grammar well and intuitively makes corrections.

We are now learning to develop ideas for organizing writing around main ideas and composing composite paragraphs. These are some things Shiva will learn in the next quarter to help him continue to grow into a mature reader and writer.

✓ ✓ ✓ ✓ ✓

3. Erin has shown excellent reading comprehension and critical thinking skills throughout this year.

She has contributed thoughtful comments during class discussions, giving evidence of her understanding of books we have read.

In addition, Erin works well in any cooperative group she is teamed with, and her strong team spirit always helps to produce great projects.

✓ ✓ ✓ ✓ ✓

4. An avid reader and prolific writer, Brent moved forward steadily in reading and writing. His ability to use context clues and inference enhanced his reading comprehension.

In writing, Brent researched prehistoric animal life and produced the book "T-Rex," which has become a "bestseller" among his peers.

Ongoing goals for Brent include developing a willingness to share his ideas and opinions in discussion, and using a louder, more expressive voice when reading and making presentations to the class.

✓ ✓ ✓ ✓ ✓

Set an appropriate goal.

5. Zach has put a lot of effort into reading during this semester, and his improved comprehension is reflected in math. For example, he can now handle word problems.

Zach has also shown responsibility with his homework. I am pleased with the reading he is doing at home and feel that this work has contributed toward the confidence he has gained in academic areas.

Zach continues to be a good friend to his classmates and is cooperative and helpful at all times.

✓ ✓ ✓ ✓ ✓

Progressive Comment

6. Jenny's confident approach to reading comes from the growing number of high-frequency words she now recognizes. In addition, she has started to rely on sound strategies for approaching unfamiliar words, using context and her own experience to predict text. This quarter she has chosen to focus on nonfiction and has read some serious European history. She contributed intelligently to our discussions on Mesopotamia and Greece.

A good listener, Jenny gives her full attention to instruction; the result is that she is able to get right to work.

✓ ✓ ✓ ✓ ✓

7. Eagerness to learn and a positive attitude have contributed to the great strides Joaquin has made in English acquisition.

In the two months since he joined our class, Joaquin has made impressive progress. He has excellent listening habits, and the result is that he has assimilated many functional words and learned to follow directions. His expanding vocabulary enables him to ask for help, and he is not shy to interact.

Joaquin is very motivated to acquire English fast and is eager to participate in all class activities.

✓ ✓ ✓ ✓ ✓

ESL

8. Stephen uses imagination and vivid description to draw word pictures. Using humor and witty dialogue, Stephen dramatizes his pieces by adding a distinct voice to his writing.

Stephen enjoys listening to and reading nonfiction. Science topics fascinate him, and he has a head for recalling facts he has learned while doing research on the Internet or with informational books. This speaks well for his level of comprehension.

Stephen's enthusiasm and effort is reflected in his work.

✓ ✓ ✓ ✓

demonstrates
Synonyms:
  gives evidence of
  shows
  performs
  is observable
  is noticeable
  displays
  indicates

9. Daphne listens attentively and therefore has a very clear understanding of directions. During writing workshop, she accepts feedback from her peers and is willing to incorporate their ideas into her writing. At the same time, she also is very thorough about giving feedback to her team members. This cooperative attitude has increased her social interaction while helping her to make significant gains in writing.

Her recent persuasion piece, "Discovering Korea," aptly demonstrated this growth. Using supporting sentences and factual information, she presented a convincing argument for the existence of two Koreas.

✓ ✓ ✓ ✓

It is beneficial to explicitly state the requirements that a good student met. It reinforces the student's and the parents' understanding of the evaluation.

10. This quarter, the subject of our integrated writing and research unit was the "adaptation and survival" genre. Jasmine chose our latest novel, *The Cay*, as the subject of her project. Her presentation, marked by clarity and detail, reflects her understanding of the genre. Jasmine's research paper contained appropriate information in well-developed paragraphs and provided evidence of her growing maturity as a writer.

✓ ✓ ✓ ✓

Progressive Comment

11. Excellent progress in reading marks Jay's work in this period. He now chooses to select something to read as a free activity and is able to sit for a while with a book.

Jay is gaining higher-order reading skills, such as analyzing story structure and determining the author's purpose.

Jay's passion for reading now extends to classics such as *Huckleberry Finn* and *The Count of Monte Cristo*.

An independent worker, Jay is focused on his work and sets high goals for himself.

✓ ✓ ✓ ✓

Useful adjectives to describe Excellent students:
  outstanding
  brilliant
  admirable
  exceptional
  wonderful
  remarkable

12. Maria's confidence is soaring these days. She listens with attention and follows directions independently. This is giving her a fine sense of achievement.

In writing, Maria made a splendid addition to our library with her picture book entitled "Robby." Her finely detailed illustrations, which included a sentence for each picture, told the adventures of her dog.

Maria has had an excellent quarter.

✓ ✓ ✓ ✓

13. Manuel has successfully authored several books this year. His stories indicate progressive development in his writing, such as a broader vocabulary and fewer errors in verb-tense agreement. Manuel expresses himself very competently, which signifies the comfort he has with the English language.

This quarter, we learned to write for a variety of purposes. We experimented with writing factual pieces, various types of poetry, and tall stories. Manuel demonstrated astonishing imagination for the tall story and created some vivid pieces, which he illustrated with care. You should ask him to show you his book titled "Tiger Two Legs."

✓ ✓ ✓ ✓ ✓

CHAPTER 3

Mathematics

THE SCOPE OF MATH HAS BROADENED greatly in the last decades. Students now practice skills in less tedious ways than the drill format. Games and puzzles help reinforce key concepts while enabling students to enjoy learning.

Problem-solving remains at the heart of math. Modern math programs create meaningful contexts for learning by focusing on everyday real-life situations that students can relate to.

This chapter includes references to math skills and concepts, but does not discuss specific topics other than the basic concepts of numeration, computation, operations, patterns, and a few others. There are frequent allusions to "math behaviors," which are part of teaching math. These behaviors include but are not limited to accuracy; checking; following a step-by-step procedure; being able to explain an answer or write how a problem was solved; and collecting, organizing, and interpreting data.

Effective math assessment tools include quick quizzes, daily mental math exercises, group projects, and games. Checklists are particularly useful in math, since so many skills might be taught within a single unit.

In the student profile for math shown below, a performance form illustrates how an ongoing recording instrument helps to create the narrative comment. Keeping written observations and forms such as these on hand reduces the need to rely on memory.

A Detailed Look at the Math Evaluation of a Capable Student: *Dylan, Fourth Grader*

Dylan would be classified as a capable student in math. Although he has problems, his learning curve shows continued growth and effort.

His teacher's notes about Dylan have been recorded on a performance form, or "tracker," which shows units that have been tackled during this reporting period along with Dylan's performance in those units. The teacher's notes on each of the areas on the tracker help her to draw up the actual report card and to compose the narrative for it. She takes many comments directly from the tracker to use for the narrative.

Performance Form for Tracking Progress

Child _____   Date _____

Individual Profile Of Progress: Math

D: Developing—Child shows some understanding, though errors or misunderstandings occur.

C: Capable—Child cannot complete the task independently.

P: Proficient—Child can apply the skill or concept correctly and independently.

E: Excellent—Child applies the skill or concept correctly and independently, and also extends and applies the skill to related math problems.

Concepts/Skills	Comments	D	C	P	E
Knows basic math operations.	Comfortable with addition and subtraction.			✓	
Computes accurately.	Quick with math facts up to eighteen.			✓	
Computes mentally.	Shows confidence in this area when working on missing addends.			✓	
Uses estimations skills.	Comfortable; had difficulty understanding vocabulary in estimation problems.			✓	
Demonstrates understanding of place value.	Found regrouping hard to understand at first, lots of practice exercises helped.		✓		
Understands fractions and percents.	Concepts are still new to Dylan. Needs individual help to guide him through.		✓		
Recognizes patterns.	Yes.			✓	
Collects, records, and interprets data.	Makes careless errors recording data.		✓		
Understands principles of probability.	Fairly good understanding, not secure yet.			✓	
Measures accurately.	Yes.			✓	
Applies problem-solving skills.	Requires individual help to guide him through.		✓		
Records and presents reasoning clearly.	Uncertain of some concepts at this time. Sometimes they seem clear to him, but when he needs to explain how he arrived at his solutions, he cannot always explain his reasoning clearly.		✓		

The Report Card, with Descriptors

Dylan's report card was filled in as shown below.

	1st	2nd	3rd	4th
LANGUAGE ARTS				
Reading Effort				
Reading Achievement				
Comprehension				
Vocabulary				
Decoding				
Writing Effort				
Writing Achievement				
Expression of ideas				
Mechanics/Usage				
Spelling				
Handwriting				
Oral Skills				
Participation				
Listening Skills				
MATH				
Math Effort		✓+		
Math Achievement		✓		
Concept development		D		
Computes accurately		+		
Problem solving		✓+		
SCIENCE & SOCIAL STUDIES				
Effort				
Achievement				
Concept development				
Class participation				
GENERAL BEHAVIOR				
Punctual and prepared				
Works independently				
Cooperates in groups				
Respects others				

Pupil: Dylan   **Grade:** 5

Classroom Teacher: Mona Melwani

Explanation Key:

  + Excellent

 ✓+ Proficient

  ✓ Capable

  D Developing

 NI Needs Improvement

NA Not Applicable

Comments   2001–2002

In spite of some problems, Dylan is working hard and growing in math.

The heart of the problem; the narrative should explain this D and suggest a solution.

Dylan's struggle in this area should be mentioned in the narrative, as it is the cause of his confusion.

The Narrative

The narrative on Dylan's report card read like this:

Dylan demonstrates a firm foundation in math facts when he computes. His mental math skills were evident when we worked on missing addends. As we moved to higher units which involved problem solving, the concepts became more challenging for Dylan.

Our units on fractions and decimals were particularly demanding for Dylan. At this time, he needs individual help to guide him through these problems. Sometimes they seem clear to him, but when he needs to explain how he arrived at his solutions, he cannot always express his reasoning clearly.

Dylan needs to practice working on fractions and decimal problems. The daily exercises that he will be bringing home will help him grow more secure in math concepts.

> *The teacher points to the area which Dylan finds difficult.*

> *Dylan's confusion and uncertainty is the focus here, with specific reference to the math units with which he is having trouble.*

> *A goal to work toward and help to attain it.*

Sample Narratives for Developing Students

1. During this quarter, we explored number patterns and rules for number sequences. Matthew understands these concepts and worked successfully on numerous pattern projects.

Matthew's computation skills continue to grow. He can identify appropriate math operations for a variety of problems. Occasionally he has trouble figuring out word problems and needs assistance. Some practice in this area will help him to gain confidence.

✓ ✓ ✓ ✓ ✓

> **understands**
> Synonyms:
> grasps
> comprehends
> figures out
> has a handle on
> recognizes
> identifies
> deciphers
> solves

2. Improved accuracy in Charlie's computation is a direct result of his willingness to take the time to check his work, instead of trying to be the first to finish.

During our unit on money, we worked on problems connected with making change. Charlie demonstrated good number sense and quick mental math in doing these problems. These same abilities give him an advantage in games and quizzes, and it is no surprise that he has proved himself to be the class "ace" in this unit.

Now he must turn his attention to fractions and decimals. These are not Charlie's favorites, because he is having a hard time grasping the concepts. As we continue to teach these concepts with numerous hands-on activities, Charlie will have opportunities to get more secure in this area.

✓ ✓ ✓ ✓ ✓

> **Positive and Negative**

3. Alison is good at breaking down complex math problems into small steps so that she can understand them better; however, her computation is not always accurate and her errors often cost her a lot.

When Alison looks for patterns, she uses models and manipulative objects to make sense of math problems. Her preference for tactile learning (using objects she can move and work with) indicates that the more practice she has with it, the better able she will be to integrate math concepts.

Alison needs to solidify her basic math facts so that she can use math operations accurately.

✓ ✓ ✓ ✓ ✓

4. Jonathan loves a challenge and approaches problems with enthusiasm. His high level of reading comprehension enables him to handle word problems with ease; however, he tends to be in a hurry and therefore often misses out on directions. This results in incorrect answers or incomplete work. Next quarter, Jonathan needs to focus on and work for accuracy rather than speed.

✓ ✓ ✓ ✓ ✓

5. Kayla's grasp of new math concepts is developing. During our units on estimation and probability, she was at first hesitant to make calculated guesses. However, as soon as she grasped a concept, she participated with enthusiasm. Overall, Kayla is tentative about math and gets nervous and confused.

While she works to the utmost of her ability, I feel that some of the concepts—especially those which involve logic and analytical thinking—are ones Kayla has not been exposed to before. Since much of this is new for her, she needs plenty of practice to meet the requirements of our math program.

Practice will also help Kayla to gain confidence in math.

✓ ✓ ✓ ✓ ✓

6. Ian attempts the challenging math problem of the day with enthusiasm but unnecessary speed. This results in some careless mistakes. I have tried to explain to him that at this time we are developing recall of math facts and are not engaged in speed work. Ian needs to slow down and check his work before submitting it.

✓ ✓ ✓ ✓ ✓

7. Oliver is competent in math. He is quick at mental computation. However, new math concepts sometimes confuse him, mostly because he is not always attentive when the concepts are being explained. Consequently, when math problems are assigned, Oliver cannot do them until he gets one-on-one assistance.

At this time, Oliver needs to focus more on the direct instruction of a lesson so that he can attend to his math assignments without extra help.

✓ ✓ ✓ ✓ ✓

8. Christine's usual cheerfulness changes when it comes to math. She becomes inattentive, distracted, and quite unhappy during math lessons. She needs to be convinced that math is not as hard as she thinks it is. Often she needs one-on-one attention in order to stay on task.

I have tried to make math more interesting for Christine with the use of physical objects and games. This does lift her mood, but only for a while.

I have now started breaking Christine's assignments into smaller tasks to help her feel that she is completing the work and making progress. Christine must continue to get this encouragement at home with math practice.

✓ ✓ ✓ ✓ ✓

> This student is clearly at an emerging level in math. Because this is a core issue for this student, the teacher has omitted any reference to other behaviors and has focused on the student's attitude as it relates to math.

9. Martin enjoys using physical objects and manipulative materials in math. His three-dimensional projects on prisms and polygons were well conceived and well executed.

Seat work is not as attractive to Martin. He resists it by trying to get it over with quickly, and so he often makes careless errors. He also does not like to do his work over when it is incorrect.

Martin cannot seem to sit still long enough to complete math exercises. He needs to settle down and focus on his work, because he is eminently capable of handling it. He distracts other students by walking around, off task. It would be constructive to talk about this matter at a meeting soon.

Meanwhile, we must encourage Martin to enjoy math by consistently using manipulatives as a reward for some seat work.

✓ ✓ ✓ ✓ ✓

> This student pushes the rules. When instructions are given, he starts ahead of the others—before his teacher has finished giving directions. He also takes short cuts, finishes fast, and calls out "I'm done" loudly. His teacher will not let him get away with incorrectly done work, and he gets frustrated when he has do things over, then sulks. His teacher has tried various strategies, but his progress is slow and she now is asking his parents to share what he gets away with at home. Together they will draw up ways to handle these problems in a consistent manner and work as a team to help him.

10. Molly has good basic math skills and is always eager to start her math work. However, word problems are still difficult for her and she seems to lose interest in these assignments. But when a problem is explained to her, she immediately figures out which operations are appropriate.

I believe Molly's reading comprehension needs to improve before she can handle word problems.

✓ ✓ ✓ ✓ ✓

11. Kelly's math skills are growing; she is now a little more comfortable with the subject, though she often needs affirmation that what she is doing is indeed correct. She works slowly but stays on task. Under close supervision, she seems to gain confidence and is able to work faster. Kelly is working at two-digit addition and subtraction.

✓ ✓ ✓ ✓ ✓

12. Simon continues to need encouragement in math. Often he is overwhelmed by the tasks before him, because he has not yet acquired enough English to understand what to do. However, he waits patiently for individual attention. We must allow him time to gain more functional language skills so that he understands directions better.

ESL

Simon listens attentively and is trying hard to do as many tasks as he can. He is shy about asking me for help, so I am encouraging him to do so.

✓ ✓ ✓ ✓

13. Robert showed understanding of basic math processes on the end-of-year math assessment tests. However, his answers were incorrect because of careless computation, which affected his overall score.

Additionally, he had some difficulty with fraction concepts. While Robert has made progress during the last two quarters, he needs further practice to build a more secure foundation in math skills.

✓ ✓ ✓ ✓

14. Jessica is competent in math. She is able to match appropriate math operations to problems, yet she is somewhat unsure of her ability. A good observer, she listens carefully as new concepts are introduced. But Jessica is nervous about attempting new problems independently and will usually ask for help.

As she gains more confidence, I hope that Jessica will begin to trust herself more. I would like to see her become confident about her problem-solving abilities.

✓ ✓ ✓ ✓

15. Yong Chu's math skills are firmly in place. His confidence with number facts and comprehension of word problems should make math comfortable for him. In fact, he does very well when he puts his mind to it. Often, however, his attention is elsewhere and his work is slow and incomplete. Additionally, he is not organized; he misplaces books and assignments.

Yong Chu needs to take more responsibility for his work.

✓ ✓ ✓ ✓

16. Julia has a good eye for patterns—an important math strategy. This term we studied percentages; Julia's grasp of this math concept is still at the developing stage. Currently she gets confused when she is asked to calculate percentages in relation to different amounts. (For example, she can easily figure out 20 percent of 100, but cannot apply that skill to 20 percent of 80.) Julia needs opportunities to practice this skill more often. Perhaps she could be asked to help figure out prices of items discounted by certain percentages at the supermarket.

✓ ✓ ✓ ✓

17. James's enthusiasm for math swings between high and low. He handles straight computation with confidence, but resists solving word problems. His reading level at this time is possibly the cause of this hesitancy. However, I believe James should attempt these problems instead of choosing the convenience of having them explained to him one-on-one.

✓ ✓ ✓ ✓

18. Johnny's confidence with math springs from a sound understanding of math operations and comfort with basic math facts. Quick and accurate at mental math, Johnny enjoys these challenges. He is less patient with written work. His presentation is messy and disorganized. Many times he has been unable to read his own work to explain how he arrived at his answer.

Johnny needs to work on producing neat, organized work and giving as much attention to pencil-paper tasks as he gives to oral work.

✓ ✓ ✓ ✓ ✓

19. Aaron has sound math skills and a competent understanding of math facts. He is well equipped to handle class assignments. However, he is often distracted and off task.

Lately, Aaron's performance has been inconsistent and he has required close monitoring to keep him from disturbing his neighbors. I shared my concern about Aaron's immature behavior at the conference we had in October, and regret to inform you that Aaron is not yet taking responsibility for his work and behavior.

✓ ✓ ✓ ✓ ✓

> This is a student with poor organizational skills. He forgets his homework, says he completes work but loses it in the mess on his desk. His assignments are late because he spends a lot of time shuffling papers, looking for his workbook, or hunting for a pencil.

20. Lionel is an excellent math student. His computation is fast and accurate. However, he does not always use his time wisely. He feels the work is too easy and will not give it careful attention. This results in avoidable errors, which he then must spend time to correct.

During work time, Lionel talks, sharpens his pencil, and occupies himself with unproductive tasks instead of finishing up so that he can move into math extension activities.

Lionel needs to be more serious about his work, and he also needs to be more responsible with his time on task.

✓ ✓ ✓ ✓ ✓

> When a teacher provides considerable detail about a student's behavior, she is telling the parents how important the issue is.

21. Mariko sometimes gets confused in math and often cannot communicate her thinking. This makes it difficult for her to explain how she solved a problem. Her basic math facts are not yet in place, and some practice will help her to feel more secure.

The math game cards that are being sent home each week should be an interesting way to help her.

Mariko is a cooperative and cheerful student.

✓ ✓ ✓ ✓ ✓

> Pointing out poor work habits and how they are affecting a student's work.

22. Nate knows effective strategies for recalling basic math facts and is now able to sort and construct two- and three-dimensional shapes with assistance. During this period, his computation has been more accurate, though he still takes a long time to complete computing assignments.

Nate is still unprepared to take part in mental math games and problem-solving discussions, and he needs some time to feel more secure in math. He often requires one-on-one support to get started on tasks. I am encouraging Nate by giving him shorter assignments so that he will experience the joy of completing his work.

✓ ✓ ✓ ✓ ✓

Whenever reference is made to poor behavior, it is best to elaborate.

23. A comfortable understanding of math operations and a high reading level are advantages that give Geoffrey a lot of confidence in math. However, this confidence does not always translate into efficient use of time. During math period, Geoffrey's attention seems to wander and he does not listen to directions, with the result that he often fails to complete assigned work.

Geoffrey needs frequent reminders to stay on task and needs to be more attentive and responsible for his learning.

✓ ✓ ✓ ✓ ✓

24. A strong math student, Ethan has a secure understanding of math concepts, and his speedy computing could make him a math star—if he stayed focused. Unfortunately, he does not give serious attention to math, because he considers it to be too easy. The result is that Ethan's math papers are carelessly done and contain many errors. Doing these assignments over again consumes time, as does his frequent talking during work time.

Ethan needs to show that he is engaged in the learning process by improving the quality of his assignments and using class time wisely.

✓ ✓ ✓ ✓ ✓

This student's poor reading ability hinders her understanding of word problems. As a result, she gets confused and loses interest. Add to this the fact that her basic math skills are not fully in place, and we have a struggling student who needs active help at home.

25. Lisa starts her math tasks with eagerness but cannot seem to sustain her interest long enough to finish up. Her math skills are not secure at this time; she is often confused when handling word problems. Further practice, along with reading problems more carefully to better understand them, will help her.

Lisa would benefit from developing a stronger, more secure foundation in math. Drills and practice at home will help.

We are also working on developing this strong foundation in class, with math games designed to do just that. Fortunately, Lisa participates in these activities with enthusiasm.

✓ ✓ ✓ ✓ ✓

26. Natalie's computational skills are better this trimester. A concrete learner, she works best with math manipulative materials, which help her understand concepts. She is not yet up to solving complex problems, and needs guidance to identify the steps they require. Her use of writing to explain her problem-solving strategies helps her understand processes, but she cannot always explain how she arrived at the solution. More opportunities for review and practice are needed.

✓ ✓ ✓ ✓ ✓

Sample Narratives for Capable Students

1. During this period, we explored patterns and relationships between numbers as a prelude to our next major unit on multiplication. Jacob participated in the activities and integrated many of the concepts essential to the next unit.

Jacob enjoys hands-on tasks more than seat work and is inattentive when written tasks are assigned. In his hurry to get it over with, he rushes his work—sacrificing accuracy for speed.

This is unfortunate, since Jacob is quite capable and can explain problems and figure out solutions. His efforts need to be more consistent. Jacob should give as much effort to his written work as he does to his hands-on tasks.

✓ ✓ ✓ ✓ ✓

Specify the behavior that is affecting performance.

2. Alexa's basic math facts are in place. During our unit on measurement, Alexa demonstrated competency as she engaged appropriate instruments for measuring weight, volume, and capacity.

Her attention to detail is also seen in the methodical way she writes down the processes she uses to solve problems. Alexa's efforts made it possible for her to catch up with assignments she missed during her recent absence.

✓ ✓ ✓ ✓ ✓

Tie student performance to instruction.

3. Jonas listens attentively, a quality which has helped him to acquire English faster. At this time, his limited English makes word problems challenging; however, when they are explained to him, he is quick to tackle the task.

I feel certain that, as Jonas gets more comfortable with language, he will approach word problems independently.

At this time, he enjoys participating in class, and math gives him opportunities to do so. Jonas is an enthusiastic learner.

✓ ✓ ✓ ✓ ✓

ESL

4. William is comfortable with math. He understands basic concepts of arithmetic and is able to identify operations needed to solve a problem. It will be helpful for William to check his work before submitting it, as he can be careless.

William is a concrete learner; he integrates concepts faster when he has models and physical objects he can use to understand an idea.

However, two- and three-step problems confuse William. We are learning to break down a problem into small steps and work at these steps individually. This approach has helped William learn to explain how he solved a problem.

✓ ✓ ✓ ✓ ✓

A weakness and how it is being handled.

5. Felicity's progress in math is indicated by the independence with which she now handles her assignments.

Her use of writing to explain her problem-solving strategies is helping her understand processes, but she needs to constantly review the processes for clarity.

Felicity has gained confidence in working as part of a team. She has a friendly, accepting manner, which makes her welcome in any group she joins. This has also raised her interest and performance in math.

✓ ✓ ✓ ✓ ✓

Progressive Comment

6. Joseph's work habits improved noticeably this quarter. He assumed responsibility for work he couldn't complete in class by volunteering to stay in at recess to finish it.

Joseph has learned to collect and organize data, and he can now interpret data using tables, charts, and graphs. He mastered the computer graphing program and was often observed helping students who were having trouble.

Joseph's self-confidence has grown along with his performance.

✓ ✓ ✓ ✓ ✓

Progressive Comment

7. Sierra demonstrated a growing interest in math this quarter. She can now recognize and create simple patterns and is able to recall addition and subtraction facts comfortably. Additionally, Sierra is now attempting the more difficult two-digit subtraction problems.

Since our last conference, Sierra's attitude appears to have grown more positive. She now seems willing to take risks and, with encouragement, she persists in her efforts.

✓ ✓ ✓ ✓ ✓

Tie in the topics in which the student did well and mention what he is tackling now. Tying in issues like this keeps parents informed about the curriculum.

8. Carlos has shown a lot of responsibility for his work this quarter. He completed assignments on time and showed that he can stay on task until an assignment is done. He is tackling double-digit addition and subtraction and is making satisfactory progress.

We are now working on division, and Carlos is having some difficulty grasping the concept. However, if his enthusiasm for math continues, I feel that Carlos will rise to the occasion and succeed, as he has with double-digit addition and subtraction.

✓ ✓ ✓ ✓ ✓

9. Sam has been more focused and attentive during this period. His math tasks have been completed on time and he is now on his way to stronger math computation. He has also been meeting deadlines for his math homework assignments.

I am encouraged by his efforts, and believe that Sam has the potential to grow into a responsible and independent worker.

✓ ✓ ✓ ✓ ✓

10. When Amelia looks for patterns and uses models or manipulative objects to understand math problems, she understands and solves difficult problems. Amelia's comfort with tactile learning (using physical objects she can move and work with) indicates that the more practice she has with this kind of learning, the better able she will be to integrate math concepts.

Amelia is a steadfast and conscientious worker.

✓ ✓ ✓ ✓ ✓

11. Anna is able to compare numbers to 1,000 using terms such as *greater than* or *less than* and *greatest* and *least*. She showed strong growth in measurement as we went through units on weight, capacity, and volume.

Although she is maintaining grade-level achievement in math, Anna's understanding of place-value concepts is not too secure. More practice will help her grow comfortable with it.

Anna is a responsible student and is caring and respectful of her classmates as well as classroom materials.

✓ ✓ ✓ ✓ ✓

12. George's growth in math this quarter was marked by the increased attention he is giving to rechecking his work before submitting it. The result has been far fewer careless errors and less time spent on corrections.

He also listened attentively to directions, and so did not need them to be repeated. Overall, George used his time wisely this quarter and was able to turn in his assignments on time.

✓ ✓ ✓ ✓ ✓

Sample Narratives for Proficient Students

1. Ben's proficiency in math can be seen in his secure understanding of math concepts. He is an eager participant in all math activities.

In our unit on using comparison symbols (< >) and finding differences between two-digit numbers, Ben confidently shared a number of strategies that can be used. He also did exceptionally well on the end-of-year math assessment test.

Ben has matured from being the shy, quiet boy who entered fifth grade as a new student to being a star performer.

Whenever possible, it is helpful to illustrate student performance with instructional goals. In this way, parents can relate to the curriculum more easily.

✓ ✓ ✓ ✓ ✓

2. Jason has developed sound competency in math and readily takes on math challenge problems.

He showed a distinct skill at identifying and building three-dimensional shapes (pyramid, cone, prism) and was able to show his understanding of the concepts correctly.

An organized worker, Jason is able to explain his problem-solving strategies by writing down each step clearly and logically. It is not surprising that other students frequently ask Jason for help, and that he is a successful peer teacher as well as a successful student.

✓ ✓ ✓ ✓ ✓

Positive and Negative

3. Brett has done exceptionally well in math this year. He welcomes a challenge and is able to apply his knowledge to solve complex math problems. Determined and confident in his math ability, Brett often attempts alternative ways of attacking a problem. By doing this, he is strengthening his problem-solving skills.

    Brett is still shy and rarely speaks in class. It would be good for him to share these strategies with his classmates.

    As an enthusiastic math student, Brett has been active in the math club this year.

✓ ✓ ✓ ✓ ✓

4. Annika attends to math with diligence. Her admirable habit of rechecking her work helps her avoid errors.

    Annika has shown strong growth during this period, comfortably handling the unit on probability and the unit on algebra.

✓ ✓ ✓ ✓ ✓

> The Good News Narrative can be elaborated to show how the student is being challenged with extension activities.

5. Steve understands concepts of multiplication and division, and handles math assignments independently.

    This semester, Steve has been on a more challenging math program. He has had to work harder to grasp new concepts. This has not been easy for him, but Steve's persistence and willingness to take risks have allowed him to accomplish a lot of tough math this quarter.

    Steve is a good model for other students to emulate.

✓ ✓ ✓ ✓ ✓

> Pointing out a student's progress through curricular content and how he has reached his goal independently.

6. Luke has passed his introductory addition math test with a full score. His progress in place value and estimating numbers indicates a sound grasp of math concepts.

    As Luke's reading ability grew, so did his ability to handle word problems. He is now working independently on them and does not need my help anymore.

    Luke's achievement is commendable for a new student who came in last semester with very little English.

✓ ✓ ✓ ✓ ✓

7. During this period, we worked on a large unit called Reference Frames, which included the use of clocks, calendars, thermometers, and number lines. We also did a unit called Patterns: Functions and Attributes. Jake

participated spontaneously in all of the hands-on activities that were part of these units. The end-of-unit tests indicated that he has developed a sound understanding of the topics on which we focused.

Jake enjoys math and is always ready to do some extra work.

✓ ✓ ✓ ✓

A Good News Narrative in which the topics covered are integrated with performance.

8. Zarina has done exceptionally well in all areas of math this year. She enjoys tricky word problems and the challenging problem of the day. She is a determined worker when she struggles for solutions, and these struggles have strengthened her math reasoning.

Our math units this quarter focused on percents and fractions. Zarina worked independently and did consistently well on the assignments.

✓ ✓ ✓ ✓ ✓

9. Halima has done exceptionally well in math this year. She often completes advanced math problems early in the week and is ready for more. Halima is not discouraged by the more difficult problems she sometimes encounters, and she willingly tries alternative strategies to discover a solution. Her determination to complete assignments is laudable.

Halima often helps students to understand problems and is a patient teacher-helper.

✓ ✓ ✓ ✓

10. Hannah's math competence is apparent when she uses more than one strategy to approach complex problems requiring multiple math operations. She also reaches solutions with appropriate mathematical thinking.

Hannah manages time better now than she used to, and makes a conscientious effort to get her work done within the allotted time.

✓ ✓ ✓ ✓

11. Megan helps herself out of difficulties in math by using manipulative models, which reinforce her math concepts. She can now calculate three-digit addition and subtraction involving regrouping. All Megan needs now is to be a little calmer with her work. She tends to either rush or panic, and both reactions cause her to make careless errors.

Always ready and eager to get started, Megan is a pleasure to have in class.

✓ ✓ ✓ ✓

This student's ability in math is not in question here, but her insecurity with math is the focus instead.

Sample Narratives for Excellent Students

The Good News Narrative

1. Navin demonstrated a secure understanding of math all year. He has done extremely well at recalling math facts and choosing appropriate operations and strategies for problem solving. His positive attitude has been a great help to those around him.

   Navin learned to figure out Fahrenheit and Celsius temperatures on a thermometer. Additionally, his handling of multiplication demonstrates how readily Navin grasps new concepts.

   ✓ ✓ ✓ ✓

It is a good idea to include a student's positive behaviors in the comment.

2. Both Victor's sound math reasoning and his talent for problem solving can be seen in the numerous graphic illustrations he uses to explain himself. He frequently shares alternative strategies for solving a problem.

   Victor's helpful attitude can be seen in his willingness to assist his classmates and unravel math concepts together with them. His cooperative attitude and hard work set a fine standard for the others.

   On the end-of-year math assessment, Victor did exceptionally well.

   ✓ ✓ ✓ ✓

All students, including Excellent students, need to be thinking about new goals and challenges.

3. Throughout this year, Dominic has displayed a secure understanding of math concepts. He is able to apply his knowledge to the various real-life scenarios with which the students are presented.

   Always well organized, Dominic records the strategies he uses in a neat, sequenced fashion. This demonstrates his clear thinking.

   Dominic is capable of doing more challenging math work, and I would encourage him to take on the math challenges that are available for any student willing to participate.

   ✓ ✓ ✓ ✓

How well the student is doing and the direction she could take next are identified here.

4. Dina has done very well in mathematics this year. Her comfort level with math allows her to use a wide variety of strategies to work through unfamiliar problems. Her performance on the money unit was very strong.

   I am surprised that Dina is reluctant to participate in our weekly math challenges, because she is very competent and could benefit from the advanced concepts she would be introduced to.

   ✓ ✓ ✓ ✓

5. Math challenges motivate Samantha, and her interest in class activities and math games is reflected by her frequent and active participation in the classroom. She is achieving her math goals with a high degree of success.

   Always cheerful and friendly, Samantha enjoys group projects and handles them with maturity. She is often the leader of her group.

   ✓ ✓ ✓ ✓

6. Lena demonstrates her sense of responsibility in the persistence with which she stays on task and completes her work. Her loud enthusiasm for group activities and her rush to get started motivate her peers as well. Sometimes I wish she would pause so that *I* can take a breath to explain the full scope of an assignment; fortunately, she does listen and waits when asked to.

✓ ✓ ✓ ✓ ✓

7. Alex's confident approach to math and his outstanding work habits combine to make him an excellent student. His math tasks are always well done and submitted on time.

Part of the fun of math comes from activities designed to integrate and strengthen math concepts. Students find these very appealing. When he is winning at one of these games, Alex can get very noisy. It is a different story when he is not. Recently I had to talk to him about good sportsmanship. I am concerned, as he is no longer finding many classmates willing to play games with him.

✓ ✓ ✓ ✓ ✓

8. Takashi is an excellent math student. He computes quickly and accurately. Because he wishes to be fast and first, trick questions can sometimes confuse him. Nevertheless, he has a good sense of humor and can laugh off a misunderstanding.

Takashi must take care to form his numbers well and present neater work. He is a friendly and cheerful member of our class.

✓ ✓ ✓ ✓ ✓

9. Christine works carefully on her math, following directions with care and aiming for accuracy. She demonstrates her growing self-confidence as she handles math problems using appropriate math operations. This quarter she learned to sort and construct two- and three-dimensional shapes. She also created graphs after collecting and organizing data.

Christine is a conscientious student and works independently.

✓ ✓ ✓ ✓ ✓

10. Stephanie's limited English makes reading directions difficult for her. As someone who was introduced to English just a semester ago, this is to be expected. However, Stephanie is not only very determined, but also knowledgeable in math. She understands math operations and has a sound grasp of math facts, which permits her to figure out directions. Stephanie does not allow her lack of English to get in the way.

Against this background, Stephanie's performance on the end-of-year assessment test can only be described as inspired.

✓ ✓ ✓ ✓ ✓

ESL

CHAPTER 4

Social Studies and Science

THE GOAL OF INSTRUCTION IN social studies and science is to develop reflective and knowledgeable thinkers. The fields of study include history, geography, government, the law, nature, and science; each is replete with key information that today's students need in order to understand the world around them. Within these areas of study, teachers choose themes that integrate critical thinking, location, research, and study skills, and other important skills.

The most common goals for social studies and science instruction are:

- ✔ To expand students' comprehension of the world.
- ✔ To help students understand relationships between humans and their physical environment.
- ✔ To explain the rights and responsibilities of citizens.
- ✔ To develop in students the skills to locate resources and to access, organize, and apply information.
- ✔ To teach scientific inquiry into the natural world.

Additionally, the ability to transfer skills learned in one unit to another is central to evaluation in social studies and science.

Among the instructional goals that are highlighted in the sample narratives in this chapter are:

- ✔ The application of research skills.
- ✔ The organization of material.
- ✔ The use of technology for effective research.
- ✔ The ability to present oral reports competently.

A Detailed Look at the Science/Social Studies Evaluation of a Proficient Student: *Brian, Fifth Grader*

The Report Card, with Descriptors

Based in large part on the teacher's notes (page 56), Brian's report card was filled in like this.

	1st	2nd	3rd	4th
LANGUAGE ARTS				
Reading Effort		+		
Reading Achievement				
Comprehension		+		
Vocabulary		✓+		
Decoding		✓+		
Writing Effort		+		
Writing Achievement				
Expression of ideas		✓+		
Mechanics/Usage		✓+		
Spelling		✓+		
Handwriting				
Oral Skills		+		
Participation		+		
Listening Skills		✓+		
MATH				
Math Effort		✓+		
Math Achievement		✓+		
Concept development		✓+		
Computes accurately		✓		
Problem solving		✓+		
SCIENCE & SOCIAL STUDIES				
Effort		+		
Achievement		✓+		
Concept development		✓+		
Class participation		+		
GENERAL BEHAVIOR				
Punctual and prepared		✓+		
Works independently		+		
Cooperates in groups		+		
Respects others		+		

Pupil: Brian **Grade:** 5

Classroom Teacher: Mona Melwani

Explanation Key:
+ Excellent
✓+ Proficient
✓ Capable
D Developing
NI Needs Improvement
NA Not Applicable

Comments   2001–2002

Brian's lively interest in science is indicated here.

Brian fell short of being excellent because he lacked a very important organizing skill that affected his writing assignments.

Brian's contribution to the class, his willingness to help his classmates, and his work behavior are recorded here.

The Teacher's Notes on Brian

✔ Brian is a fifth grader with an astonishing curiosity for science topics.

✔ He read independently on the topics we focused on this semester (electricity, simple machines), and contributed interesting information as we read and discussed these topics.

✔ To answer his many questions, I directed Brian to resources where he could locate answers. He seems to use these resources well.

✔ By the end of the first semester, Brian was a resource for students who wanted information, as well as for those who needed help locating information.

✔ Brian is helpful and willing.

✔ Brian's advanced research skills and his high level of interest in the subject put him at a proficient level in science.

✔ What he now needs most is to learn to organize his work better. Because he gathers so much material on a topic and wants to use all of it, the volume of information becomes cumbersome to manage and painstaking to put together.

✔ Brian completed most of the objectives planned for these two units. His group projects were well done and he explained various machines, including levers and pulleys, with confidence.

✔ Brian's written assignments were disorganized and required a lot of one-on-one time to help him discern what was important to keep in and what needed to be left out. Making such determinations is an important skill that Brian needs to develop.

The Narrative

Based in large part on the teacher's notes above, the narrative comments accompanying Brian's report card read like this:

Brian has an astonishing curiosity for science topics. His search for information often takes him to the library and Internet. His independent reading on the topics we handled this semester (electricity and simple machines) indicates a high reading level.

Brian's interest in science is linked to instructional goals; the ability to search for information; a high reading level; and independence in learning.

Writing assignments create a predicament for Brian. He gathers a tremendous amount of information on a topic and is eager to use it all. The result is that the material becomes too much to handle, and Brian has trouble organizing it. We spent some time together one-on-one, going through data and questioning which of it fits into the requirements of the assignment. Having chosen the material, we then worked to organize it so that it reads well. This was not an easy process for Brian. However, the ability to select and prioritize information is a skill he must continue to work on and develop further.

Brian's struggle with an important research and writing skill is described, as is the way in which he was helped.

Brian was a helpful resource to his classmates during this period. Students often asked Brian to help them find information, and he was always willing to help and share.

The narrative ends on a positive note—showing how Brian shares his expertise.

Sample Narratives for Developing Students

1. Geena produces good work when she puts her mind to it. Generally, she cannot seem to sustain her interest for long. She starts excitedly, contributing ideas and thoughtful comments during discussions. However, when it is time to implement those ideas, she seems unable to do so.

Geena's written reports do not have the required completeness and depth expected in fifth grade. Her report on citizenship and her project on the first Americans were both disappointing.

To encourage Geena to stay focused on her written assignments, I have paired her with a partner in the hope that the shared responsibility will persuade her to sustain her effort. I am optimistic that this will work and will observe the pair carefully.

✓ ✓ ✓ ✓ ✓

This is a good example of tying behavior to a specific content-related assignment. Notice that the teacher also mentions how the behavior is being handled.

2. Nico's research reports give evidence of his fine observation skills. His recent report and illustrations on plant life show his ability to add interesting details to make an attractive report. However, he is not very willing to present or share his reports. He does not take part in discussion and is inclined to be quiet.

I have encouraged Nico to speak up and give his opinion on issues we discuss, and I hope to hear him soon in our group meetings.

✓ ✓ ✓ ✓ ✓

Positive and Negative

3. Connor has had a good year. He has shown growth academically, and many of his assignments show the fine work he is capable of. His eager participation in the unit on rain forest animals culminated in the visual account he presented of the food chain. It is unfortunate that Connor cannot always sustain this performance. His inconsistency stems from his habit of putting off for tomorrow what he can do today. Consequently, Connor had several late assignments this quarter. The hurriedly done work he creates in an attempt to catch up is not as complete or detailed as it needs to be.

Connor needs to work on time management skills so that he learns to allow sufficient time to produce good work.

✓ ✓ ✓ ✓ ✓

Compare the work of the student when he is focused and when he is not. If you can find a reason for this inconsistency, mention it.

4. Rachel joined in our weather unit activities with enthusiasm. A cooperative member of her group, she shared her ideas and helped with illustrations. Rachel was not as excited about writing her weather reports. She also was not able to answer questions on clouds and precipitation, indicating that the underlying concepts relating to cloud formation and weather changes were unclear to her. Accordingly, she did not do well on the unit assessment.

Rachel needs to be more engaged in the objectives and purpose of the activities.

✓ ✓ ✓ ✓ ✓

5. Science and social studies are not Kieva's favorite subjects. She is not motivated to do the reading and planning required for our various activities.

As I mentioned when we met in January, Kieva has a hard time working in a group because she is unwilling to accept the ideas of other group members. If her ideas are not used, she often sulks and walks out of the group. Our goal in group projects is to develop teamwork and cooperative efforts.

This quarter Kieva agreed to do a project all by herself, but she seemed to tire of it and could not complete the assignment. We worked together one-on-one to finish it, and she seemed to understand that sharing the job makes it easier.

✓ ✓ ✓ ✓

6. Juan's attitude toward class tasks needs to improve. He has trouble concentrating and does not always listen. As a result, when he needs to get started with work, he does not know what needs to be done. Juan was not prepared for his presentation about the ocean floor, and his participation in the group project was minimal.

I am concerned about Juan's attitude and lack of enthusiasm.

✓ ✓ ✓ ✓

7. Ethan shows curiosity about the world and wants to do all of the reading and writing that the tasks in class demand. At this time, however, his limited reading skills make it difficult for him to read and write about many concepts. He does listen and understand, though, and we are focusing on vocabulary development and simple sentences to help him expand his skills.

Ethan demonstrates respect and care for materials and works well with his peers.

✓ ✓ ✓ ✓

8. Andrea is learning to listen to directions more carefully. This has improved her performance; she was, for example, able to complete her report on strange animals of the rain forest. Additionally, she participated in the group project on medicinal plants of the rain forest.

Andrea's oral work is getting better, and I've noticed that she practices reading her reports so that her soft voice can be heard.

At this time, Andrea's written reports tend to be short and not very well developed. Although she locates information from library sources and the Internet, she is not able to find the material she wants. Even after she is guided to find the right material, she is uncertain of how to use it. As the class continues to work on these data-gathering skills, I will be encouraging students to read more non-fiction to help them understand the purpose of informational texts.

✓ ✓ ✓ ✓

Just the Right Words: 201 Report Card Comments • Scholastic Teaching Resources

Sample Narratives for Capable Students

1. Esther's writing improved this quarter. Her report "How I Became a Cloud" showed careful organization of material and an understanding of the concepts we are learning. The detailed illustrations that accompanied her presentation were well executed and showed her commitment to the project.

Esther is reading more and is now able to speak confidently and share her opinions. It is evident that she is developing an awareness of the world around her.

✓ ✓ ✓ ✓ ✓

The Good News Narrative

2. It has been a pleasure to have Lila in my class this year. She has had a successful year and has grown both socially and academically. She is now taking part in interactive activities and has developed good organizational skills.

It would be helpful for Lila to prepare for the extensive reading to come in the year ahead. She could do this by widening her interest in reading to include a variety of genres and informational texts.

✓ ✓ ✓ ✓ ✓

Point to an area the student can work on.

3. Paul learned to successfully integrate technology in his report on oil spills. The advances he made in his computer skills include discovering more maps, web sites, and new parts of the electronic encyclopedia. These discoveries helped Paul gather more visual information on the effects of oil spills on the oceans.

The more important learning arose from the fact that Paul was so involved with what he was discovering that his mass of information grew beyond manageable limits. He had to make difficult decisions about what information he should use and what he should discard.

✓ ✓ ✓ ✓ ✓

Point to the student's innovative integration of technology.

Pick on a specific project or assignment in which the student showed developing skills.

4. For the endangered animals unit, Theresa chose to do a project on whale hunting. She worked hard, enlivening her project with interesting facts about whale hunting equipment, which fascinated her classmates. The report required collecting information and then organizing it, a process that was sometimes frustrating for Theresa. However, she stayed on the job and was proud of her completed project.

✓ ✓ ✓ ✓ ✓

5. Emily is aware that she needs to improve her writing skills, and she is willing to work harder to achieve this. During recess, she comes in for extra help in sorting out her ideas and finding ways to express them clearly.

I feel certain that with her strong motivation, Emily will acquire the writing skills she needs.

✓ ✓ ✓ ✓ ✓

Positive and Negative

6. Gino has an eager curiosity about the world. As our current events unit comes to a close, Gino is beginning to relate cause and effect to the events of the world. He also is showing a real interest in science. The experiments with magnets fascinated him. He understood the concepts and was able to write about the results of his experiments in an organized way.

Gino is quiet; he rarely shares his opinion or critical views about topics we discuss in class. However, when encouraged (or pushed) to do so, his comments indicate that he is listening and that he understands. I would encourage him to participate more and be willing to risk sharing his views.

✓ ✓ ✓ ✓ ✓

ESL

This student enjoys learning; he is active, curious, and works hard. The parents should be told how he is handling his second language and how he is performing, including mention of areas for further growth.

7. This quarter Eli has been an enthusiastic participant in map-reading activities, especially figuring out latitude and longitude. He excelled at the science project on solids, liquids, and gases. Using diagrams and labels to explain his understanding of these elements, Eli was also able to work on experiments independently.

Although the vocabulary and the concepts we explored were challenging, Eli rose to the occasion—even with his limited English—and did exceptionally well.

✓ ✓ ✓ ✓ ✓

8. Michele worked hard to research and write her biographical report on Louis Pasteur. Using the organizational approaches we have been learning, she included details of Pasteur's life and times. Her work reflected a true understanding of the importance of careful organization. The classroom applause at the end of her presentation on Pasteur was well deserved and gave her reason to be proud of herself.

I hope this success will excite Michele and spur her to produce even more quality work as we move into our next unit on sound and light.

Michele does not always use classroom time wisely, but it is heartening to see what she is capable of when she puts her mind to it.

✓ ✓ ✓ ✓ ✓

Sample Narratives for Proficient Students

1. Alicia's awareness and understanding of the world are growing as she continues to read nonfiction related to our topics this quarter: rights and responsibilities of citizens and global interdependence.

Her research project, "Our Changing Earth," explored the socio-economic effects of floods and droughts. She presented her report with photographs and supporting statistics.

Throughout all of the units of study we focused on, Alicia was an active participant in small and large group activities. One of the important things

Identify the important curriculum goal that is the student's current focus.

she learned is the need to use more than one source when researching answers to questions.

Alicia shows enthusiasm for learning and has a cheerful attitude toward schoolwork.

✓ ✓ ✓ ✓ ✓

2. Lee enjoys learning about the world around him. During instruction time, he volunteers to answer questions and always has interesting news to share. He has developed a tremendous bank of background information on the topics we are studying.

Lee's space exploration project, "On the Moon," reflects his ability to locate resources and discern what information to put in a report and what to leave out. His final report demonstrated his understanding of the concepts we explored during this unit.

Lee displays an excellent attitude and always puts forth his best effort.

✓ ✓ ✓ ✓ ✓

3. Judith has shown herself to be competent in dealing with the concepts presented in our units on inventions and ocean animals.

She takes part in discussions and is not afraid of sharing her opinions and insights. These critical-thinking skills will support her reading, which continues to improve.

Judith's strong interest in and developing knowledge of global events are beginning to give her a perspective on world events. She comes prepared to share some news from the newspaper each day.

Judith is a good class citizen, willing to share and help with classroom duties.

✓ ✓ ✓ ✓ ✓

Progressive Comment

4. Colin's passion for knowing the answers to many science questions compels him to read a variety of books. At this time, he has developed solid background knowledge on the solar system. He has no trouble understanding science concepts and can explain them intelligibly.

Our study of the Second World War kept Colin interested in Europe for a long time, and he had a lot of enlightening and interesting contributions to make during group discussion.

Colin has done commendable work this quarter.

✓ ✓ ✓ ✓ ✓

The Good News Narrative

5. Our study of political systems required students to read informational texts on different types of governments. As we read these texts and connected them to world events, Shin Yi developed a strong global perspective on events in the news. His growing comprehension of the world around him prompted him to ask several questions which continue to occupy our research and discussion.

Shin Yi is a thoughtful and sensitive boy who has a caring attitude toward those around him.

✓ ✓ ✓ ✓

6. Mikayla shows curiosity about the world and is hungrily reading about the history of London. She has gone beyond the class requirements to find out more about London's past. In the process, she has discovered the delights of tracking down information on the Internet.

Mikayla has become quite proficient in locating information. The next step for her is learning how to efficiently use that information: how to choose the data most relevant to the topic, and how to order her research in an interesting manner.

These are skills we will learn in the weeks ahead. I feel certain that Mikayla will develop essential critical-thinking skills in the process.

✓ ✓ ✓ ✓ ✓

7. Leah is an active participant in social studies discussions. She understands the concepts of natural phenomena and interdependence, but because she is sensitive to environmental issues, she cannot believe what people are doing to the rain forests. As we move further into political systems and world economics, she may find some answers.

In the meantime, Leah continues to read about the wealth of our forests and continually emphasizes the importance of recycling to her classmates. I believe Leah has the makings of a responsible world citizen.

✓ ✓ ✓ ✓ ✓

8. Our social studies unit this quarter was about limited world resources and interdependence. Although Lidia does not have enough English at this time to fully understand instruction or to express herself comfortably, she finds ways to participate in the activities.

Lidia works hard to learn vocabulary and always has a dictionary on her desk. She listens carefully, observes keenly, and is not afraid to ask questions. And the illustrations she hands in give every indication that Lidia grasps the concepts we are learning. They are carefully drawn, exquisitely colored, and appropriately labeled.

Lidia displays enthusiasm and keenness for learning, and has a positive attitude toward school.

✓ ✓ ✓ ✓ ✓

Mention the student's growing awareness and developing leadership skills.

9. Shaina, always active in our social studies class, brought bright ideas and enthusiasm to our unit on endangered animals. Sensitive to environmental issues, she brainstormed with her group and together they came up with awareness ideas to help save trees.

Shaina's involvement with the recycling project gave her the opportunity to lead her group. Together they shared readings and statistics and made a wonderful presentation at the school assembly.

Shaina is beginning to understand the relationships between humans and their physical environment.

✓ ✓ ✓ ✓ ✓

10. Grace truly enjoys working on group projects and being part of a team. These projects have brought out her leadership skills. She shares responsibility and contributes to the management of the project.

For the unit on volcanoes and earthquakes, Grace was prepared with appropriate background reading. She shared valuable information in the class.

Grace's final project, called "Riches from Lava," was well researched and planned. Her beautiful artwork and diagrams for this project clearly illustrate the kind of detailed, hard work Grace can accomplish.

✓ ✓ ✓ ✓ ✓

> This student's motivation must not only be commended, but also illustrated with a specific example.

Sample Narratives for Excellent Students

1. Jamal's curiosity about the world was stimulated by the facts of ecology and world climates. He made an effort to read books on these topics independently and came prepared to join in the discussions.

Jamal is a self-directed worker and can be relied on to figure out directions and resources independently. Working cooperatively with a group of three classmates, he helped to investigate the Russian steppes and present a grand mural which communicated the group's clear understanding of life in this region.

Jamal is a diligent and conscientious worker.

✓ ✓ ✓ ✓ ✓

> This student's excellence is supported by a number of examples: reading ahead on the topic, cooperative group work, and investigation of the topic.

2. That Daniel's favorite subject is space was made clear when he joined in creating space modules with partners and explained scientifically what they could do. His active participation in our study of space prompted him to explore space history electronically. He exercised his computer skills to create visuals, which he used to explain advances in space science.

Daniel's frequent choice of reading books on space as a free activity was further evidence of his interest in this topic. During this period, Daniel's reading performance improved, and he learned to be analytical about what he read.

✓ ✓ ✓ ✓ ✓

> It helps to show how different subjects and skills fit into an interdisciplinary unit. Here, the study of space in the subject area of science also included the use of technology, the study of history, and extensive reading.

3. Our unit on world events engaged Kim totally, and her knowledge of the impact of global events has grown. Although we have now moved on to other topics, Kim continues to expand her awareness of the world around her. At this time, she is quite an expert on Croatian politics.

Kim's high level of reading and comprehension allow her to work independently, and her interest in non-fiction continues to sustain her interest in global affairs.

✓ ✓ ✓ ✓ ✓

4. Ava has done superior work this quarter. Her interest in this quarter's topic—changes in the earth's surface (erosion, weather, and landslides)—was particularly passionate, as she identified how the seaside town where she lives was irreparably affected by erosion.

Ava's fondness for reading expanded into informational books this quarter. She was able to identify and recall details of the causes of erosion and how weather contributed to it, and she communicated her understanding effectively.

An independent worker, Ava is focused on her tasks and consistently produces fine work.

✓ ✓ ✓ ✓ ✓

5. Ming has shown an aptitude for science and was engaged in science texts on heat and light for most of this quarter. This year he has developed the skills to formulate scientific questions and conduct a fair test.

Having learned to use instruments accurately, Ming discovered that assumptions and conclusions must be tested by scientific methods. He conducted experiments to test the properties and characteristics of heat. His methodical preparation and execution of these experiments, along with his careful recording of his findings, show how serious Ming is about science.

✓ ✓ ✓ ✓ ✓

6. This quarter, students learned how to identify an area they wanted to study, examine what information was needed for the topic, and figure out where that information could be found. We then brainstormed the best way to organize information

Gregory chose to study animal behavior in the polar regions and launched into extensive reading on the subject. For his final assignment, he chose to produce artwork and accompanying text which communicated his understanding of interdependence in nature effectively.

Gregory is a mature student who reflects on what he reads and learns.

✓ ✓ ✓ ✓ ✓

7. This quarter Jeffrey learned how to make correct use of a compass and a map key, and how to use letter/number coordinates to interpret a map.

Jeffrey's ability to conduct research was evident when he used numerous resources—including the library, encyclopedias, videotapes, and the Internet—to investigate mummies. Additionally, he learned to use historical evidence to support his writing in his report called "The Curse of the

Mummy." Jeffrey's technological know-how was engaged fully when he chose to present his report as a slide show.

Jeffrey's inquiring mind drives him to reach innovative ideas, which extend his skills and knowledge of the world around him. This is a wonderful asset.

✓ ✓ ✓ ✓

8. Our Space unit is always popular with third graders, but this year the ideas, images, and projects that students initiated were particularly splendid.

For his space project, Matt read about scientists and learned about scientific processes. Then he shared what he learned from his reading by creating an imaginative machine for use in spaceships for medical research.

Matt's flair for scientific inquiry is exciting and his inspired presentation was admirable. I hope you are prepared for Matt's desire to continue his research in a space ship one day!

✓ ✓ ✓ ✓

> Integrating social studies, language arts, and work habits.

9. Henry continues to maintain a high level of interest in social studies and science. Our unit on space exploration this quarter was really exciting for him. His spontaneous participation and cooperative teamwork were particularly evident when he took responsibility for team jobs as a considerate team player.

Most recently, Henry successfully researched the emergent layer of rain forest life. He learned the importance of using more than one source of information as he searched through a variety of reference books, maps, and the Internet. The final product he presented was a fascinating piece, wonderfully illustrated, about the food chain in the emergent layer.

✓ ✓ ✓ ✓

10. It has been a pleasure to have Nina in my class this year. She is cooperative and helpful at all times. Her mature social skills make her a valuable organizer for group projects.

Nina's project on magnets contained a number of activities that the students were able to try. She was able to answer questions about how the "tricks" worked.

It is clear that Nina did an extensive amount of independent reading, because her report was well planned and well presented.

✓ ✓ ✓ ✓

> Point to specific skills the student is gaining.

CHAPTER 5

Social/Emotional Behavior and Work Habits

THIS CHAPTER EXAMINES STUDENT behaviors and work habits. Goals for students in these areas include self control, self discipline, a sense of responsibility, and the ability to work independently. Of course, few students enter school showing maturity in all of these qualities. Schools are precisely where students learn appropriate work and play behaviors, and where they are continually developing socialization skills. Both on the playground and in the classroom, students' social interactions offer clues to

their personalities. Teachers observe and guide students' actions and reactions, with the objective of steering them toward more socially acceptable and academically sound habits.

With this in mind, this chapter has been organized to reflect the evolving nature of human behavior. Accordingly, the three categories used here are Needs Improving, Improving, and Capable, which replace the categories used in the other chapters—Developing, Capable, Proficient, and Excellent.

Sometimes, particularly when class size is large, teachers may not notice small improvements in behavior occurring over a period of time. The result is that a student who, in the teacher's mind, has been labeled negatively early in the year never has the chance to be "untagged." For this reason, a checklist for each student—one that is initiated at the beginning of the year and maintained at regular intervals—can afford the teacher a more objective and comprehensive perspective. Such a tool can be very helpful in tracing student progress in behavior and work habits.

A Detailed Look at the Social/Emotional Behavior and Work Habits Evaluation of a Needs-Improvement Student:
Eric, Fourth Grader

The Teacher's Observations of Eric

Eric, a fourth grader, has poor organizational skills. His work space is always cluttered and his desk full of things he collects. And he collects everything: papers, stickers, comic strips, pencil stubs, bits and

The Report Card, with Descriptors

Based in large part on the teacher's observations (see pages 66 and 68), Eric's report card was filled in like this.

	1st	2nd	3rd	4th
LANGUAGE ARTS				
Reading Effort		D		
Reading Achievement		✓		
Comprehension		✓		
Vocabulary		✓		
Decoding		✓		
Writing Effort		D		
Writing Achievement				
Expression of ideas		D		
Mechanics/Usage		✓		
Spelling		✓		
Handwriting		D		
Oral Skills		✓		
Participation		✓		
Listening Skills		✓		
MATH				
Math Effort		D		
Math Achievement		D		
Concept development		✓		
Computes accurately		✓		
Problem solving		✓		
SCIENCE & SOCIAL STUDIES				
Effort		D		
Achievement		✓		
Concept development		✓		
Class participation				
GENERAL BEHAVIOR				
Punctual and prepared		NI		
Works independently		NI		
Cooperates in groups		✓		
Respects others		✓		

Pupil: Eric **Grade:** 5

Classroom Teacher: Mona Melwani

Explanation Key:

- \+ Excellent
- ✓+ Proficient
- ✓ Capable
- D Developing
- NI Needs Improvement
- NA Not Applicable

Comments   2001–2002

These Ds must be explained in the narrative in terms of Eric's poor work habits and organization.

Eric's disorganization is shown here, along with how it reflects on his work in other areas.

pieces of erasers, etc. Messy folders hold Eric's class work, projects in process, and assignment sheets—which are so folded and disorganized that he can't recognize them even when he sees them. He is often confused due to these messes. This must change, because Eric is spending too much time looking for things he knows he has but cannot find. Eric's work quality is suffering.

In order to make any plan for helping Eric truly effective, his parents need to be involved.

The Narrative

Based in large part on the teacher's observations above, the narrative comments accompanying Eric's report card read like this:

Eric is eager to work and does wonderful work when he attends to it, but lately he has been unable to work with the care required. A lot of his time is lost looking for a pencil or eraser or misplaced work papers.

The positive note is tied into Eric's problem.

Eric's crowded work place and cluttered desk are an inconvenience he cannot handle by himself. Because he loses his work and sometimes has to do it over, his assignments are either submitted late or are sloppily done. His science assignment on how clouds are formed is a case in point. His three-page project was incomplete because he misplaced two of those pages. Numerous math worksheets he's had to do over are another example.

The teacher explains with specific examples how it is affecting Eric's work in different areas.

Better organization is our goal for Eric. He and I have worked on a plan to help him achieve this. The "to do" list we created together outlines his tasks for the day and will be checked daily. Labeled folders to hold his papers are now in place and will be checked every week.

What the teacher is doing and how the teacher and Eric are working together to solve his problem.

A similar list is being sent home so that you may help him check his school bag and homework assignments. With our combined efforts, I feel certain that Eric will be productive and better prepared for school each day.

The parents are made part of the plan so they know how to help him, too.

Sample Narratives for Needs-Improvement Students

1. Alison appears attentive during instruction time and will often ask questions in an effort to understand things better. However, when she gets back to her desk, she is usually uncertain of the directions for getting started. It would therefore appear that, although Alison seems to be attentive, she is not really listening.

The increasing number of careless errors Alison is making on assignments further supports my impression that her mind is elsewhere. I have encouraged her to double check with me before she starts her tasks so that she knows exactly what she has to do.

Our goal for Alison in the coming quarter is for her to stay focused so that she can handle directions correctly.

✓ ✓ ✓ ✓

Positive and Negative

2. Corey is confident about his knowledge of the world; his strong oral skills and wonderful imagination make him a treat to listen to. He shares his views, his understanding of the books he reads, and his personal adventures with an enthusiasm that is delightfully entertaining.

The only thing that slows down Corey is seat work. Writing and note-taking do not hold Corey's attention; he becomes both distracted by and distracting to those around him. Many of his written assignments are carelessly done and remain incomplete.

Corey and I have made a plan to reward him on completion of his written work.

✓ ✓ ✓ ✓

3. Sean's most endearing quality is his willingness to help others in class. Unfortunately, he might be going too far with this, as it sometimes takes away from the time he could be using to complete his assignments. Sean and I are working together to help him understand that not every call for help needs to be attended to, and that sometimes it is best for students to figure out things by themselves. I believe that our efforts will be effective—especially because Sean has had to miss recess twice this quarter to complete tasks.

This student has never heard of the concept of time management. He spends a lot of time staring into space or doing the least important things first. His teacher has been working with him in many ways, including teaching him to prioritize tasks.

✓ ✓ ✓ ✓

4. Beth's seat work continues to be slow. As our workload increases, it will be necessary for her to keep pace and be self-directed.

Beth seems to lose track of the task before her and needs reminders to keep working on it. Her work is frequently submitted a few days late and even then it is incomplete.

The school counselor and I have worked out a plan with Beth to help her get started and to stay on task until she is finished. The plan is to reduce task requirements for her so that she can complete them within a shorter time. When she is ready, we will extend the tasks so that she gets into the habit of staying focused for longer stretches of time.

This student's pace of work is pointed out along with the behaviors that cause her work to be slow and late. An effective plan to help this student should include her parents and involve at least one parent conference.

✓ ✓ ✓ ✓

5. Shy and quiet, Chloe rarely shares or contributes in class. Even during show and tell, she only "shows" and does not "tell" about what she has brought.

To make her feel comfortable, I have teamed Chloe with two class-mates and assigned all three of them a class job each day. I am hoping that this will give her a sense of participation and some friendships as well.

✓ ✓ ✓ ✓

6. Ray is not very serious about his work. His assignments are incomplete and untidy. He does not like to do them over. In order to make schoolwork more manageable for him, we have, in consultation with the school counselor, simplified assignments for Ray so that he can do them in a shorter time and feel a sense of achievement for completing his work. We are monitoring his progress.

✓ ✓ ✓ ✓

Progressive Comment

7. This quarter Jason has made a tremendous effort to control his anger and frustration. He has tried very hard to hold back his tears and to avoid sulking. When he has succeeded, it has felt like a victory for both of us. While there is room for further improvement, I am encouraged by his efforts. Your support has been valuable and I appreciate it.

✓ ✓ ✓ ✓

8. A motivated student, Robert has a fine grasp of academic tasks—which he completes well and on time. He needs to develop a similar maturity in his social behavior.

Robert's spirited participation in math games and interactive reading activities is inclined to be loud and distracting. On these occasions, he has had to be contained, sometimes with a time out. His impulsive behavior also got him into trouble twice this quarter, once when he pushed a class-mate and once when he cut in the lunch line.

We are working on a plan to help Robert be more aware of his actions and to offer positive reinforcement whenever he succeeds. It will be beneficial for Robert to have a similar plan at home, and I would be happy to discuss this with you whenever you're available.

✓ ✓ ✓ ✓

9. Ari is slowly beginning to understand class expectations. He now raises his hand when he wishes to speak, and he also waits his turn to get my attention. However, he has had to stay out of recess twice during this period for pushing students in the lunch line and for jumping in line.

We are monitoring Ari to remind him about acceptable behavior.

✓ ✓ ✓ ✓

10. Courtney has difficulty listening. Often she asks questions even before I have completed giving the instructions. This habit not only interrupts the smooth transfer of directions to Courtney herself, but distracts the rest of the class as well. It is not surprising that Courtney seeks extra help frequently. She often cannot finish her assignments on time and needs to be supervised closely to encourage her to complete her work.

✓ ✓ ✓ ✓

11. Youssef enjoys a high level of popularity among his classmates. His cheerful nature and sense of humor are truly endearing, although I notice he is not finding it easy to handle this popularity. It takes time away from his work. In the recent math exercises involving interactive problem solving, Youssef's reduced attention produced poor quality work. In addition, written work he submitted was sloppy. Youssef stayed in for two recesses to complete the job.

Sample Narratives for Improving Students

1. A kind friend and a good class citizen, Jim helps with class jobs like organizing books and putting materials away. He is always available to lend a hand to his friends when they need to clear their homework folders and bags; however, he needs to work on organizing himself as well. Jim helps his friends clear their desks, but his own is a mess.

✓ ✓ ✓ ✓

2. Johari is an excitable second grader whose enthusiasm runs ahead of her; she can become very noisy at these times and gets off task.

Johari's reading and writing levels indicate that she is very capable; however, she gets busy watching others and cannot complete her tasks on time. We are working together on self-control and staying on task.

✓ ✓ ✓ ✓

> Specify the problem behaviors that are affecting the student's work.

3. Owen showed improved time on task and completed his work in the allotted time. He has not had to spend any recesses in the classroom. On a few occasions, he even finished them ahead of time.

I am happy to report that Owen's homework assignments are now coming in regularly. Thank you for your help with this.

✓ ✓ ✓ ✓

Progressive Comment

4. Academically, Mariel is making steady progress; she approaches her assignments with confidence and works hard at giving her best effort. She also participates well in classroom discussions.

Socially, Mariel is somewhat reticent. She usually cannot find someone to be her partner in paired work. I have also observed that she plays by herself during recess. As the year goes on, I hope she will develop new friendships among her classmates, especially because she has not yet tried to do so.

✓ ✓ ✓ ✓

5. Although Michael usually gets to work as soon as assignments are explained, in recent weeks I have noticed that he takes some time before starting his work to visit with his neighbors. This slows him down, and he has been failing to complete class work.

Michael is a capable student; we must ensure that he uses his ability to the fullest.

✓ ✓ ✓ ✓

Progressive Comment

6. Abe's work habits improved this quarter. He brought in his homework regularly and seemed to have actually read the books he took home. His attention to instructions is better, and he does not have to come to me for help.

✓ ✓ ✓ ✓

7. Alberto, always cheerful and well mannered, is eager to get started on tasks even before all of the directions have been given. Consequently, he will sometimes misunderstand what needs to be done. Often this means having to start the assignment all over again.

✓ ✓ ✓ ✓

There is a natural progression in this comment. The teacher points out the student's strength, his weakness, and how it is being addressed.

8. Nick has plenty of confidence when it comes to math, and deservedly so. Nonetheless, he rushes into math tasks with an excitement stemming from his belief that he knows how to do it, and that the task is easy. This habit causes avoidable errors, which misses the whole point about accuracy in math.

Nick is aware of the difference between knowing how to do something and working at it carefully, as he has had to give up some play time to redo his work.

I feel certain that these experiences will teach Nick the value of rechecking—a word he now has glued prominently on his desk.

✓ ✓ ✓ ✓

Positive and Negative

9. Alexis's caring attitude toward her classmates and her support for them made her a real asset to the class. She is always willing to share, to help clean up, or to run an errand. Although this willingness to take responsibility is admirable, Alexis needs to prioritize and make sure that good citizenship does not take time away from her work. She needs to allow herself adequate time to do her best on assignments.

I believe Alexis could have done a better job on her writing assignments and could have kept up a healthier reading log if she had done so.

✓ ✓ ✓ ✓

10. Terry gets nervous when we share views as a whole class. He shies away from asking or answering questions. I believe he needs time to gain self-confidence so that he can participate.

✓ ✓ ✓ ✓

11. Always willing to give his best effort, it is surprising how often Kyle misses details that have been described and needs them to be explained a second time.

   To help Kyle concentrate and stay attuned to instructions, I often ask him to recall the instructions just given. This is helping; however, there is room for further improvement.

   ✓ ✓ ✓ ✓

12. Shy and soft spoken, Janell is not yet ready to participate fully in class. She appears to be following directions when they are explained, yet she sits quietly, not knowing what needs to be done—and is unwilling to ask. Many of Janell's assignments remain undone. When they are explained a second time, one-on-one, she does get a start. In the meantime, however, a lot of time has been lost.

   To help Janell feel a sense of completion in her work, I have shortened her tasks. Further, she and I have agreed on some cues that I will give her to remind her to start work.

   ✓ ✓ ✓ ✓ ✓

> State the problem and how it is being handled.

Sample Narratives for Capable Students

1. Jeremy's progress in academic areas continues to improve. He participates in class activities, listens, and follows directions well. Jeremy always tries to do his best, and produces good quality work on time.

   ✓ ✓ ✓ ✓ ✓

2. Christopher's growing maturity is seen in the numerous friendships he is developing and in the leadership role he is playing on group projects. His team spirit and consistency of effort are most evident during class projects such as building pyramids and designing machinery.

   ✓ ✓ ✓ ✓ ✓

3. Isabel is cooperative and works well in a group, doing her share of the jobs and more. Organized and neat, her workplace and her work are always tidy. Isabel extends this respect to the care of classroom materials.

   ✓ ✓ ✓ ✓ ✓

4. Ved participates in class discussions, often making thoughtful contributions to the topic.
   Helpful and mindful of his classmates, Ved is much sought-after by his many friends.

   ✓ ✓ ✓ ✓ ✓

5. Joshua has gotten over his initial shyness. He now raises his hand and volunteers to share. In addition, he presented two reports to the class on behalf of his group. Joshua practiced delivering his report so that he spoke less hurriedly and with a clear voice. The presentation was well received by his classmates.

✓ ✓ ✓ ✓

6. Clarence is a cooperative student with many friends. His conduct makes him a positive role model for the entire class. He has been supportive of others and has a great sense of fair play.

✓ ✓ ✓ ✓

7. Ashwini has tried hard to stick to the rules. She has been better about waiting her turn at the water fountain and when she needs the teacher's attention.

✓ ✓ ✓ ✓ ✓

Progressive
Comment

8. Class work done on time and only two missed homework assignments are the evidence of Tom's improved attitude toward school.

This quarter proved that when Tom puts his mind to it, he can produce good work.

✓ ✓ ✓ ✓

9. During Writer's Workshop, Erica listens attentively to the ideas of others and also provides important feedback.

She shares her opinions confidently and feels comfortable speaking in any situation.

✓ ✓ ✓ ✓

Time Savers*

Social/Emotional Behavior and Work Habits: Useful Phrases

a constructive quarter

a pleasure to have in class

accepts criticism constructively

attentive and conscientious

big improvement on last test

completes and submits homework punctually

converses well, but written work is careless

could be good if only he/she worked more carefully

daily work has been haphazard and often of poor
    quality

demonstrating improving attitude

difficulty working with others

displays organizational skills

does not complete assignments in the allotted time

does not use time wisely

easily distracted

effort is inconsistent

exhibits consistent self-esteem

fails to complete assigned class work

fails to finish independent assignments

follows directions

forgets instructions and directions

gaining more self-confidence

good classroom helper

good oral work but written work could improve

inattentive

is a steady worker

is caring toward friends

is unprepared for class (work materials)

keeps up with homework

maintaining grade-level achievement

makes careless errors on assignments

needs close monitoring

needs more effort/concentration

needs some help to organize materials

needs to come for extra help

uses time wisely

needs to have high standards for him-/herself

needs to take the time to edit, correct, and perfect work

not working to capacity

observes school rules

participates actively in class

participates enthusiastically

participates often

pays attention

respects class rules

respects classroom materials

respects property

room for further improvement

seeks extra help frequently

seems more engaged in class

sets excellent example for peers

should be more serious about his/her work

should practice reading with expression

shows interest in her work but lacks confidence

shows understanding of material

submits work on time

takes pride in written presentation

though he/she made progress, is capable of better
    work

uses time wisely

warm and sensitive

work improved this quarter

works cooperatively with others

works faster under close supervision

works independently

* Useful phrases for the other subject areas are located in Appendices C, D, and E, pages 92–94.

CHAPTER 6

General Comments

THE GENERAL COMMENT IS most frequently used by homeroom elementary-school teachers. Homeroom teachers often rely on general comments because they teach multiple subjects and are therefore aware of a student's performance in many areas.

The general narrative is a kind of global comment; as such, it is particularly handy for students who are doing well in everything. For these students, there are no particular issues to draw attention to. (This is not to imply that excellent students should be treated casually. It is always a good idea to mention especially good work, since students read their own report cards and should see the encouragement they deserve.)

Nonetheless, the general comment can also be used if the teacher wishes to draw attention to a problem. If this is the case, it is best to focus the general narrative on only that issue, because this indicates to parents that the issue is important. The general comment need not exclude information about a student's fine performance in other areas; the goal is simply to avoid embedding the problem in details about many areas, which might cause it to be missed altogether.

Thus, in summary, the general comment is most typically used by homeroom/regular elementary classroom teachers and most comfortably suited to students who are doing well across the board. However, it certainly can be used effectively by other teachers and for other kinds of students. It is the care with which it is written and applied that counts.

The general comments in this chapter are organized into three categories: Developing, Capable, and Proficient. Because a student may not be developing in all areas, and could be doing better (capable) in another and already be proficient in yet another, the comments here lend themselves to "mixing and matching"—that is, to combining appropriate paragraphs or sentences to report on different levels of progress.

A Detailed Look at the Use of General Comments for a Second-Grade Student: *Jennifer*

The Report Card, with Descriptors

Based in large part on the teacher's notes (see page 78), Jennifer's report card was filled in like this.

	1st	2nd	3rd	4th
LANGUAGE ARTS				
Reading Effort		✓		
Reading Achievement				
Comprehension		D		
Vocabulary		✓		
Decoding		✓		
Writing Effort		✓		
Writing Achievement		D		
Expression of ideas		NA		
Mechanics/Usage		NA		
Spelling		✓		
Handwriting		✓+		
Oral Skills		✓		
Participation		D		
Listening Skills		✓		
MATH				
Math Effort		✓+		
Math Achievement		✓		
Concept development		✓		
Computes accurately		✓		
Problem solving		✓+		
SCIENCE & SOCIAL STUDIES				
Effort		D		
Achievement		D		
Concept development		D		
Class participation				
GENERAL BEHAVIOR		✓		
Punctual and prepared		✓		
Works independently		D		
Cooperates in groups		✓		
Respects others		✓		

Pupil: Jennifer   **Grade:** 5

Classroom Teacher: Mona Melwani

Explanation Key:
- + Excellent
- ✓+ Proficient
- ✓ Capable
- D Developing
- NI Needs Improvement
- NA Not Applicable

Comments   2001–2002

Jennifer's low reading level is reflected here.

Jennifer is very new to the writing process as it is practiced in this classroom, so her skills in these areas are inadequate. However, the teacher decides on NA and does not mention writing in the narrative comment because she feels that for now it is a priority for Jennifer to improve her reading.

Jennifer's effort in math is acknowledged here.

The effect of Jennifer's reading level is seen here as well.

Jennifer is well behaved. On the whole, her work is below grade level and she does not possess the skills to interact confidently. She hesitates to ask for help.

The Teacher's Notes on Jennifer

- ✔ Jennifer is a shy, quiet student. Not very secure among her classmates, she is one of those children who tend to come out of their shell slowly.

- ✔ During sharing time, Jennifer prefers to say that she has no news rather than to draw attention to herself.

- ✔ IRA and formal reading assessment indicate that Jennifer is reading below grade level, (1.2. first grade, second semester level). This assessment took place at the end of the first semester in second grade.

- ✔ Jennifer's low reading level points to why she is performing below grade level in areas such as writing and social studies.

- ✔ Jennifer needs one-on-one help to get started with her work.

- ✔ Jennifer is encouraged when she gets things right.

- ✔ Math seems to be Jennifer's strength. She seems very comfortable with mental math exercises, and has even raised her hand a few times to respond during math exercises.

- ✔ Jennifer has grasped concepts of regrouping in subtraction with three-digit numbers.

- ✔ Jennifer works well on multiplication and division facts.

The Narrative

Based in large part on the teacher's notes above, the narrative comments accompanying Jennifer's report card read like this:

Shy and soft-spoken, Jennifer is progressing in some areas better than in others.

In math, Jennifer identifies the appropriate math operations for solving problems. Her grasp of regrouping in subtraction with three-digit numbers and her understanding of multiplication and division facts indicate good math sense.

> The report begins with a positive note on Jennifer's math skills.

Jennifer's performance in reading and in social studies are both matters of concern. The recent reading assessment test and the informal reading inventory both indicated that Jennifer is reading below grade level. This situation is affecting her work in social studies. Some help in this area would go a long way toward getting Jennifer interested in the topics that we focus on, so that she can begin to acquire the skills and vocabulary of this subject.

> The single most important goal for Jennifer is to improve her reading, so her teacher chooses to focus on this one goal.

The books Jennifer will bring home to read to you are intended to help develop her reading further, so that she can follow directions and work independently.

> Jennifer's difficulty with social studies texts is connected to her reading level.

Sample General Comments for Developing Students

1. Max is so eager to launch into work that he begins before he has heard all the directions. Consequently, he misses out on many of the details of the task.

This quarter, he has had to do a few math exercises and a project on ancient cultures over again because he did not follow directions.

Haste also causes Max's work to be sloppy and his handwriting illegible. He is more capable than this work indicates.

Our goal is for Max to approach his work in a less hurried manner and to listen to directions carefully. To this end, Max is now being asked to repeat the directions before he starts.

The improved quality of his work will give Max a sense of achievement and pride.

✓ ✓ ✓ ✓ ✓

Focus on the important concern. How it is affecting the student's work, and what help is being given?

2. Shy and soft-spoken, Lara is not yet ready to participate in classroom activities without a lot of encouragement. Often she sits quietly unaware of what needs to be done and is unwilling to ask.

The recent assessment test indicated that Lara is reading below grade level and needs some support in this area. The books she will be bringing home to read to you are intended to develop her reading further so she can follow directions independently.

I am encouraging Lara to come up and ask me for help instead of waiting for me to come to her. Perhaps you could mention this to her as well.

✓ ✓ ✓ ✓ ✓

Describing the behavior that shows lack of independence drives the point home.

3. Alyssa has settled into class routines and is now aware of seat work as a time to stay on task and complete assignments.

Working on the plan designed to help her, Alyssa wrote a book report on The Baby-Sitters' Club. She also presented facts about polluting emissions in our unit on the environment. This is a good start on the research skills she must build in order for her reports to have more content.

We continue to learn ways to develop writing ideas and organize them. As Alyssa integrates and practices these skills, she will be able to make steady progress in her writing.

✓ ✓ ✓ ✓ ✓

Make connections between past and present performance. For a student who may be having a hard time, draw attention to what lies ahead.

4. Lance gets along well with his classmates. He is always willing to help in the classroom and befriend shy students. In a large group, Lance gets nervous and shies away from asking or answering questions.

Although comfortable in math, Lance's attention sometimes slips. The quality of his math exercises in particular has been inconsistent. He did good work on the projects related to shapes and patterns, but did not do as well on place value.

Lance needs to develop more confidence so that he can participate more often. He also needs to stay alert on his tasks.

✓ ✓ ✓ ✓ ✓

5. Teresa remains unengaged in class. She rarely participates in classroom discussions, as she is often distracted doing something else—something totally unrelated to our class task. Often she is not aware of the task at hand.

At this time, Teresa is falling behind in math and has not been able to keep up with the social studies fact report on volcanoes.

Teresa's work habits are a matter of concern, since she can't seem to get work done and needs constant reminders to get on with her tasks.

Assignments have now been made shorter for Teresa so that it is easier for her to pay attention and finish small segments at a time.

My concerns regarding her academic performance, reported to you in our fall conference, continue.

✓ ✓ ✓ ✓ ✓

These two comments (5 and 6) are appropriate only if the teacher has already shared her concern with the parents in person.

At such a meeting, the teacher should support her view with work samples to show exactly what is meant. It is also fair to find out if the other teachers who meet with the student have similar concerns.

6. Abby has not been able to complete many of her language and math tasks this quarter. During direct instruction (just before assignments are given), Abby distracts herself and her neighbors by talking. Because she does not listen when it is time to start work, she does not know what to do. I have had to point this out often to her.

As I mentioned at our conference in March, we have broken up class tasks into smaller assignments for Abby so that she feels the success of completing work. However, Abby has not been able to perform these smaller assignments. She often interferes with her neighbors' work instead of attending to her own.

My concern for Abby continues. She seems to need constant supervision and is not making much progress.

✓ ✓ ✓ ✓ ✓

Positive and Negative

This comment focuses on both the student's progress in reading and how it is demonstrated, as well as on behavioral problem areas that continue to need attention.

7. Cynthia's enjoyment of reading is a positive development this quarter. Her term book reports demonstrate her improving comprehension and writing skills.

In the weeks to come, Cynthia needs to work faster, as she has not been able to complete all of her assignments in math and writing. Her unit project on oceans is still due.

Cynthia needs to learn to use her time wisely. If she stays on task and does not allow her social interactions to interrupt her, she will have plenty of time to complete her work.

✓ ✓ ✓ ✓ ✓

8. Sayeed enjoys writing and has many stories to tell. At this time, he spills his story out—writing quickly without thinking about sequence or development. Although we have already learned about story structure, we will continue to practice it.

Currently, we are learning how to develop a story using storyboards to help create story lines with a beginning, middle, and end. Sayeed needs to keep his mind on these concepts.

I observe that Sayeed is as hurried in math as he is with his writing. In his excitement—"I know how to do it" and "It's easy"—he races to be the first to finish and makes careless errors. This causes him to miss the whole point about math accuracy.

Sayeed needs to slow down. He needs to understand instructions and work through the problems carefully.

✓ ✓ ✓ ✓ ✓

Focus on the one habit that's causing the problem.

9. Natasha has many ideas for stories, which she shares orally with excitement. When it comes to composing, however, she finds it difficult to organize her material and loses all of her initial excitement. This then discourages her.

This quarter, we created a storyboard pattern to help Natasha write her stories step by step. I will be observing her progress as she practices with this structure.

Natasha's problem may just be that she hurries to get done and, consequently, overlooks important details. At this time, I have to often remind her to read the directions over again so that she follows them correctly.

Natasha needs close supervision. Perhaps it will help if she practices doing her homework by reading directions and following the steps with an adult.

✓ ✓ ✓ ✓ ✓

This student has many problems; she may be young for her class, immature, or just have poor concentration. Notice that each problem is followed by what has been done to help the student. The parents are asked to help as well.

10. Tony is slowly developing as a reader. He now demonstrates one-to-one correspondence and recognizes that words are separated by spaces.

In writing, he takes great care in forming his letters and can recognize most of them. The concept of inventive spelling—putting together the appropriate letters to make the sounds of the words he wants to write—is still not clear to him.

In math, Tony is beginning to understand concepts of addition and subtraction. At this time, he is demonstrating his understanding with math materials like blocks and dominos.

Although Tony still requires support, he is willing to work hard and gives each task his best effort.

✓ ✓ ✓ ✓ ✓

A homeroom teacher may wish to mention a student's performance in more than one area. Here, three areas are handled in three short paragraphs.

Sample General Comments for Capable Students

Integrate curricular content with performance.

Suggest a way to help.

1. Lucy follows directions with care and works well with her peers in group activities. Her writing skills improved noticeably as she successfully integrated our lessons on combining sentences and punctuation in her own writing.

In math, Lucy is able to identify math operations for simply-stated problems, which she works on with accuracy. However, math games and problem-solving activities which require the application of these operations tend to confuse her. This is an area we will continue to work on in the next quarter.

In the meantime, more opportunities to practice word problems and games will help her.

✓ ✓ ✓ ✓

Acknowledge parent help.

2. Vivi has made significant strides in reading. These strides are evident in her ability to read directions and to grasp math word problems, which she handles competently now.

Steady progress in all curricular areas marks Vivi's progress this quarter.

I am pleased with the help you are giving her at home, and feel the support you have extended has contributed to her improvement.

✓ ✓ ✓ ✓

Progressive Comment

3. Jodi's approach to work is organized. She follows directions with care and can be depended on to do a neat and accurate job.

Jodi's understanding of math concepts has improved overall this quarter. As we move into double-digit addition, I find she sometimes feels overwhelmed. Perhaps some practice and encouragement at home will provide opportunities for Jodi to overcome her fear.

A good worker and a wonderful friend, Jodi is a pleasure to have in class.

✓ ✓ ✓ ✓

Changing sentence length gives a flow to the writing that makes it more readable.

4. Tamara has settled into second grade with ease. She is excited about work and school, and reads and writes at grade level.

Strong decoding skills using context clues and visual clues aid Tamara's comprehension when she reads science texts as well as math directions. She is slowly gaining in math vocabulary.

Tamara is comfortable with basic math operations. Double-digit subtraction and place value occasionally challenge her. This unit includes numerous activities and opportunities to practice, and I feel certain that Tamara's persistence will prevail.

✓ ✓ ✓ ✓

5. Elizabeth continues to develop and grow in reading and math. As her understanding improves, her written responses are getting better. This was particularly noticeable in the science experiments she recorded and the creative writing project she produced after our study of literature in the fantasy genre.

Encouraged by her success, Elizabeth's curiosity on the properties of water (our science unit) encouraged her to locate more resources on the Internet.

This has been a good quarter for Elizabeth.

✓ ✓ ✓ ✓ ✓

6. Luis's spirited participation in class activities this quarter is evidence of his growing confidence. He now volunteers to recite his poems and is willing to take on math challenges without fear of failure.

During our study of prime numbers and factors, Luis was able to use multiples, primes, and square numbers to solve problems.

Luis demonstrated initiative when he volunteered to explain the feeding habits of Orca whales to the class. His improved interest in academic areas is encouraging.

✓ ✓ ✓ ✓ ✓

7. Richard's strengthening oral expression is noticeable when he explains his understanding of a story and shares insights about the author's purpose.

Writing tasks continue to be a struggle for him. Richard and I have designed a storyboard format that will help him to organize his ideas. As he continues to practice with the format, we will monitor his progress.

✓ ✓ ✓ ✓ ✓

8. A broken arm has not prevented Marina from attending to her classroom assignments. She used her time well while staying in during recess, completing her social studies project on the Great Barrier Reef and doing math corrections.

In spite of her injury, Marina has remained cheerful and conscientious about her work.

✓ ✓ ✓ ✓ ✓

9. Tyler enjoys poetry and remembers the weekly poems with ease. He takes pleasure in reciting them in class, bringing a lot of feeling and zeal to his readings. He is always willing to extend himself in reading and writing, though not in math.

Tyler's reluctance with math continues. He struggled with decimals, particularly multiplication. He is a capable boy, but somewhat nervous with numbers. He is now working with a partner to help him along. I am also sending work home so that he can practice.

✓ ✓ ✓ ✓ ✓

---

develop
Synonyms:
acquire
advance
build on
enlarge
expand
extend
get better at
grow
increase
move up
move ahead
progress
raise
widen

Specify how the student is being helped.

10. Ana continues to respond positively to her school experiences. Her comfort with the English language makes her a fluent reader and an imaginative writer. She organizes stories well and understands the concept of story development.

Ana is maintaining steady progress in all academic areas.

Socially, Ana is making new friends and getting along well with her classmates.

✓ ✓ ✓ ✓ ✓

Make clear exactly what
the student needs to
practice.

11. James's persistent attitude and general cheerfulness endears him to his peers and teachers alike. A hard worker, he tries his best in all learning situations—even when he does not always find the subject matter easy.

James is making progress in handwriting. Practice has improved his handwriting, and he should continue to work on it by paying attention to forming letters clearly and allowing spaces between words.

✓ ✓ ✓ ✓ ✓

ESL

12. A quiet, diligent student, Alexander works in the reading support group with eagerness. At this time, he is making excellent progress in math. He takes pride in his work and strives to do his best.

Alexander's determined effort in reading has encouraged him to read a lot, but I am not sure whether he understands all of what he reads. It may be better for him to slow down and figure out the new vocabulary he meets. He still has trouble understanding text at this grade level and needs individual instruction.

Always cooperative and helpful, Alexander is a conscientious worker.

✓ ✓ ✓ ✓ ✓

Use the core of the
comment space to zero
in on the issue that is
affecting the student's
work.

13. Reading aloud is a special pleasure for Henry, and he often volunteers to do so. It is a delight to listen to him as he reads with expression, putting himself fully into the story.

Although Henry works hard, he sometimes misses instructional details for language arts and social studies assignments, which then need to be explained to him individually. This frequently takes time away from the task and Henry has had to stay in twice during recess this term to complete work.

Henry's progress in math has been consistent. This quarter he did very well in estimation, place value, and telling time.

✓ ✓ ✓ ✓ ✓

14. Our readings of *The Story of Helen Keller* and *The Stories Julian Tells* have fascinated the students this quarter. Bernardo was quite engaged with these stories. He learned many new words, which he tries to use in his writing.

In math we covered fractions, multiplication, and division. Although Bernardo did satisfactorily on them, I believe he is capable of doing even better. He just needs to pay a little more attention to how he works out math problems. Occasionally he will miss a step and thereby miss the solution. Getting more comfortable with multiplication facts will impact his progress positively.

Bernardo has had a good year, and I have enjoyed having him in my class.

✓ ✓ ✓ ✓ ✓

15. Claire enjoyed our readings of *Louis Braille* and *Ramona Quimby, Age 8*. Her interest has led her to read other biographies.

At this time, Claire continues to require support in composing quality answers to questions in our social studies units. She is not very enthusiastic about doing research or presenting a careful study of the topic she chooses.

I am particularly concerned about Claire's inability to work in a group. Her reluctance to work cooperatively and share in the work often leaves her with no option but to do a project all by herself.

I have talked to Claire about this, and we are working on strategies (which I shared with you) to help her get along with her peers and to do her part. I am happy to report that, in a recent activity, she worked with a partner and showed an improved attitude. This effort is encouraging.

> Review the problem and how it is being handled. When you involve a parent, as in this case, it is important to give feedback.

✓ ✓ ✓ ✓ ✓

16. There is a noticeable improvement in Jared's attitude toward learning. He is completing class tasks within the allotted time, and he missed only two homework assignments during this period.

In math, he explained to the class the variety of strategies that can be used to solve subtraction problems, and was quick to figure out counting by 11s.

The writing exercises Jared submitted show that he is integrating the rules of punctuation we are learning.

Jared's performance proves that, when he puts his mind to it, he can turn out good work.

This has been a productive quarter for Jared.

> **Progressive Comment**

> **noticeable**
> Synonyms:
> seen
> evident
> clear
> apparent
> observable

✓ ✓ ✓ ✓ ✓

17. Rory is beginning to assume responsibility for task completion and is feeling a sense of achievement. Her progress has been reflected in her performance in language arts projects and math, as well as in her report on the duck-billed platypus.

Rory now chooses to read books without pictures and is happy that she can read "books with lots of words." At this time, her reading is on grade level.

During this period, Rory attempted the math challenge program for the first time. Although she could not handle all of the problems, she appears determined to keep trying. She also moved up to a new spelling list. Rory has good reason to feel proud of herself.

> Report changes in student behaviors that are helping.

✓ ✓ ✓ ✓ ✓

Sample General Comments for Proficient Students

1. A reliable student, Aparna listens to directions and follows them with care.

An outstanding performance of *The Cat in the Hat*, staged by Aparna's group, demonstrated the cooperation and respect she brings to working with her peers. Aparna's enthusiasm makes group projects a lively task for all involved.

Aparna especially enjoys our math games and our daily math challenges. Quick to identify strategies that work with the games, she uses her problem-solving skills to figure out math challenges.

It is not surprising that Aparna is popular among her classmates, as she has a positive attitude and a cheerful manner.

✓ ✓ ✓ ✓

> Support your statement with a specific example.

2. As a student new to English, Lo does not always find it easy to understand instruction and follow directions. However, he listens attentively and attempts the assignments by watching others.

Lo has acquired enough English during this period to ask for help from his classmates. He also comes to me to check if what he is doing is correct. All of this points to his growing comfort with his new school and new language.

Lo's enthusiasm and desire to do all the work is admirable.

✓ ✓ ✓ ✓

> Track the progress of an ESL student in small steps.

> ESL

3. Amy's spontaneous participation in activities keeps her fully engaged. Writing stories and reading about science topics are her favorites. As you know well, Amy gets so excited about her ideas that she is unaware of how noisy and distracting she can be. This quarter, she has had three time outs on such occasions to help her calm down.

Yet at the same time, Amy shows a lot of maturity in her written assignments and in her homework. Her reading log is evidence of her careful recording of the books she has read and her thoughts about them.

Amy recognizes that she needs to work on controlling herself, and she is trying.

✓ ✓ ✓ ✓

> Even a high-achieving student might have some behavior that needs correcting, and it's all right to mention it. This may not be news to the parents.

4. René continues to develop and grow in all academic areas.

Our social studies units on the rain forest and Egypt have motivated René to read nonfiction books. She is fascinated with animal life and the natural phenomena surrounding these forests. Her excellently executed mural demonstrates her understanding of the rain forest

This has been a constructive quarter for René.

✓ ✓ ✓ ✓

Just the Right Words: 201 Report Card Comments • Scholastic Teaching Resources

5. Douglas came to third grade with a fine ability to read and a secure knowledge of math facts. Since his grasp of reading material is high, he reads and understands word problems and directions with ease. He is therefore able to work independently on advanced math lessons.

During whole-group sessions, Douglas contributes to discussions appropriately. When we discuss the literature we have read, he shares his views and insights. These indicate a sound understanding of the text.

Helpful and mindful of his classmates, Douglas is much sought after by his many friends.

✓ ✓ ✓ ✓ ✓

The student's strength is used to highlight two important curricular areas with his behaviors woven in.

fine
Synonyms:
    good
    competent
    satisfactory
    well-crafted
    pleasing
    acceptable
    suitable
    at grade level
    high-quality

6. Notable strides in spelling and math describe Adam's progress this quarter.

Adam's spelling scores have gone up and he is now approaching more challenging words. In math, Adam sailed through decimals and percents comfortably.

During this period, Adam has come in every Monday ready with his weekly poem, which he recites in class without causing himself embarrassment. This is a positive development, and your support has been helpful in achieving this.

✓ ✓ ✓ ✓ ✓

7. Liam is settling into third grade with ease. An attentive listener, he follows instruction and directions with care. His reading and math skills are comfortably in place, and he approaches these curricular areas with confidence. He also enjoys writing and loves to share his stories.

Liam works well independently. He has proved himself to be a responsible and cooperative member of the class.

✓ ✓ ✓ ✓ ✓

The Good News Narrative

8. Stephen has done remarkable work this quarter in math and language. His reading has taken a leap forward and he is now devouring chapter books at great speed.

Stephen works very well in collaborative groups and often takes a leadership role. Most of all, he loves a challenge and is motivated to attempt math challenges and spelling quizzes. His enthusiasm for school and his participation make him a good model for other students.

✓ ✓ ✓ ✓ ✓

The Good News Narrative

9. Science is obviously Miguel's favorite subject, and he has developed a store of knowledge on various science topics. He shares the information and communicates it appropriately during class discussions.

In math, Miguel has done well in the areas of estimation, place value, and telling time. A goal for Miguel would be to strengthen his multiplication tables.

✓ ✓ ✓ ✓ ✓

10. Bonita is maintaining steady progress in all curricular areas.

She is moving forward steadily in math and can be relied on to figure out math problems independently. Her high level of interest in our study of the insect world motivated her to read many reference works on the subject. Bonita's enjoyment of reading is reflected in the remarkable reading log she keeps. In it, she eagerly shares her views on the books with a great deal of perception. The log also reflects the variety of books she is reading now.

Bonita works hard and puts forth her best effort in class.

✓ ✓ ✓ ✓

11. Gwen enjoyed our unit on autobiography. Her book reports on *The Story of Helen Keller*, *Marie Curie*, and *Louis Braille* were comprehensive. Further, working on the reports generated a lot of enthusiasm for reading, and Gwen is now choosing to read more biography.

On the end-of-year math tests, Gwen did very well. Her performance on fractions, multiplication, and division was praiseworthy, both for her speed and for her accuracy.

Gwen demonstrates an excellent class attitude and always puts forth her best effort.

✓ ✓ ✓ ✓

Show growth with specific examples and tie it to instruction.

12. The 22 books Asif read this quarter are a sure sign of his commendable reading effort. He also tested above grade level on the independent reading inventory.

The mature understanding Asif brings to literature contributed to his insightful responses to our social studies readings on Squanto and the founding fathers of America.

When Asif reads aloud, he may be somewhat nervous, as he tends to stop and start often. This affects the smooth flow of the text. I would encourage him to read aloud to you each evening. The practice will help him to be more comfortable and to achieve fluency.

Asif is a cheerful student and gets along well with his peers.

✓ ✓ ✓ ✓

Show how progress in one area is supporting another.

Identify a problem and suggest help to overcome it.

13. Scott is actively engaged in the learning process. His project on the Chippewa Indians was well researched and written.

Scott has brought in all of his homework assignments this quarter and has maintained his home reading log, filling in both the name of the book and the comment section as required. You will recall that this was something he neglected to do last term.

✓ ✓ ✓ ✓

Indicate improvement by comparing it to past performance.

88

Appendix A: The Generic Paragraph

The generic comment is distinct in two ways:

i) It is meant to be used for all students in one grade. For example, Mrs. X teaches social studies in fifth grade. The school she teaches in has three fifth-grade classrooms totaling 70 students. Each of the 70 report cards will have the same generic opening paragraph, which will spell out the curriculum covered in that period. Mrs. X will then add an individual comment to each student's report card to describe how that student performs.

ii) The generic comment is content specific. That means it is typically used by a content-area teacher. Of course, such teachers are more common at the middle- and high-school levels, but it is not uncommon to have one or two subject teachers in primary school, too. For instance, co-curricular subjects like P.E., music, computer, art, and so on are often taught to a whole grade or even a whole small school by one teacher.

Generic paragraphs are helpful to teachers and parents alike. The teacher gets to focus on what units were taught, the skills covered by them, and the established criteria for checking how students are integrating those objectives. For the parents, it is a clearer connection between what was taught, for what purpose, and how their child is doing.

The danger in generic starters is that they can get overloaded with curricula content and have little to say about the student's performance. Teachers need to remember to keep a balance.

The paragraph explaining the objective of the units will usually be positioned at the start of the comment section followed by the student's progress in the areas mentioned. Following are samples of how these paragraphs can be structured.

Language Arts

1. Our literature focus this term was on the biography genre. After reading a number of famous biographies of historical figures, students worked in small groups to discuss the salient characteristics and purposes of this genre.

The final writing project required students to choose one biography for in-depth study. The project integrated both reading and writing skills.

In writing, they had to learn to summarize sections of the text. They also had to read extensively to evaluate and interpret text against historical facts.

Neena's project on Anne Frank…

2. In writing this term, we have emphasized the use of specific word choice and the place of metaphors and similes in a particular piece. We read a variety of books to discern how authors created word pictures with the precise use of language.

The students then chose a number of topics and practiced applying metaphors and similes in their own writing. We extended word choice to include color words, sound words, and feeling words to develop a bank of descriptive language the students could employ to develop their writing ideas.

Yvonne wrote a fine description of her pet cat…

3. Language structure is a major unit in fifth grade. It embraces many sub-topics, which we handle in gradual steps.

Our strong focus on writing in this grade requires the students to have a thorough understanding of the mechanics: capitalization, punctuation, paragraphs, and spelling. These are important tools for good writing, as well as for purposes of self-editing.

We first practiced these skills with a variety of drills, and then students practiced editing their drafts to improve their earlier written pieces. This is an area we will continue to work on to ensure that students integrate these mechanics in their own writing and reduce the editing task on their drafts.

Sheila was quick to make corrections in the drills we did. However, when it came to editing her own work, she could find no errors till they were specifically pointed out to her.

4. In reading, the students have been exposed to a vast selection of literature. Students read selected books as a class choice, others as a group choice, and still others as an individual choice.

Two purposes are served in reading a variety of literature. The first is to expose the students to the ever-widening world view. The second is to develop awareness of the various genres, styles, and language that authors use.

The group discussions, tasks, and projects provided students with opportunities to express their thoughts and respond to the ideas of others. It also gave them the responsibility of sharing the reading assignments.

Harry's love of reading led him to read books on a number of interesting topics, such as…

Math

1. We began the year reviewing familiar concepts about data collection, interpretation, and graphing. We later extended our focus to include classification and attributes. Students worked on addition and subtraction strategies, applying this knowledge to solve more complex multi-step problems.

Selena's comfort with date collections and her ability to graph with confidence is seen in…

2. This quarter we explored patterns and relationships between numbers with the use of manipulative tools and models. The activities included grouping objects in multiples and adding. This foundation is being laid for our next big unit on multiplication.

John demonstrated…

3. In third grade we encourage students to reflect on what they have learned by writing down the processes they use in approaching math problems. In this way, they clarify their thinking and are able to reason out their solutions to math problems.

During this period, we covered word problems involving addition and subtraction up to 18.

Meredith worked hard on some challenging math problems involving…

4. In fifth grade, arithmetic concepts and mathematical thinking are fostered in numerous ways. The math morning meeting starts with the "problem of the day." Next, a range of group and individual problem-solving tasks are assigned. These are aimed at making mathematics more meaningful. Finally, hands-on activities are promoted to aid understanding.

These daily opportunities allow students to explore and discover patterns, practice computational skills, and draw connections among math operations.

Jana is comfortable with…

Social Studies

1. During this period, students investigated the transportation systems and history of medieval England. Our visit to the Transport Museum and the video, "The First Railways," prepared the students for the field trip to the local railway station.

The unit involved a number of important study skills, such as reading maps, figuring out schedules, purchasing train tickets, and negotiating transfers. The impact of transport on the economics of villages was explored.

The unit culminated with each student researching and presenting a topic.

Rachel's project, "The Railways and English Cottage Industries," demonstrated…

2. Our science unit explored the relationships between depth and water pressure, the effect of friction on movement, and the motion of ocean waves. Our projects integrated writing, computer applications, and mathematics.

The study expanded to include scuba diving, submarines, and the comparison of the weight of water against a variety of oils.

Students had to do an individual project and participated in a group project as well.

David's individual project on…

3. Third-grade science began with a study of matter—including space, volume, mass, weight, and density—and how it relates to the forces of gravity.

Students discovered facts about air and water pressure and surface tension with a number of experiments. They learned to write their findings in a proper format.

During this unit, the help of parent volunteers was very important. We appreciate the help that so many of you so willingly gave.

Sylvia demonstrated her experiment on surface tension with the use of...

4. In social studies this semester, we identified topic maps, such as climate maps and grid coordinates, for the four climatic regions. Students learned to use these coordinates to look at latitude and longitude.

Our focus was an in-depth study of the tropical rain forest. Students investigated and researched the unique flora and fauna of these regions and the wealth of products the rain forests produce.

Two projects were assigned to each student. One was an independent project on the adaptation of people and animals to their environment. The second involved working with partners to examine the use or materials in our own environment that ravage the rain forest, and how we can help protect it.

Both projects integrated language arts and math, as well as art and computer classes.

Colin's independent project on the iguana showed...

In his group project with Sherry, the topic was paper...

Appendix B: DO'S AND DON'TS
...to keep in mind when writing narratives

DO be specific; have student samples before you when reporting about difficulties the student is experiencing.
DON'T rely on memory or just one example of student work to assess progress.

DO cite specifics such as "She talks out of turn," or "He does not do his share of work in group projects."
DON'T make judgmental statements such as "His conduct is bad," or "Her work is not good."

DO offer one or two specific suggestions for the parent to follow up with at home to help the student.
DON'T choose more than one (or a maximum of two) goals for improvement.

DO paraphrase: "This year we will use math manipulatives, which are physical objects that allow students to experience math in other ways."
DON'T use educational jargon or acronyms such as *whole language, six traits*, SATs, ACTs, IEPs, *paradigm, inclusion*, or *immersion*.

DO keep plenty of student work and ongoing notes on the students to help evaluate progress.
DON'T wing it.

Appendix C: Time Savers

Language Arts: Useful Phrases

asks perceptive questions to improve understanding

beginning to use new words learned in class

can make generalizations about character, setting, plot

can spell common words accurately

chooses to select something to read as a free activity

compares different kinds of literature

decoding still difficult

determines problem and solution

exhibits reading-like behavior

essays lack progressive development

enjoys listening to books

enjoys listening to nonfiction/chapter books

enjoys/participates in shared reading experiences

follows directions

gets lost in long sentences

good spelling both in daily work as well as on tests

handles books correctly, with care

handwriting is difficult to read

has learned to use cursive handwriting neatly

has mature approach to reading and writing

has shown some interest in revising and editing work

identifies letters of the alphabet (upper/lower)

identifies main idea

inconsistent use of capitals at beginning of sentences

incorporates new vocabulary in writing

incorrect use of quotation marks

interested in books on…

is able to edit work independently for punctuation and grammar

is able to express feelings and share opinions

is able to use contextual clues to get meaning from text

is a fine oral reader

is developing an inferential understanding of text

is developing reading strategies

is gaining confidence as his/her vocabulary base widens

is learning to make notes and collect information before writing

is now volunteering to participate in class

is showing more focus in reading and writing

is showing some gains in fluency with text

joins in with shared reading

knows words are separated by spaces

letters are well formed and work is neat

limited and repetitive vocabulary

listening and speaking vocabulary has improved

listens carefully

makes choices to read during free time

needs assistance to choose appropriate reading materials

needs more reading practice

needs to edit work for simple errors of punctuation

paragraphs not indented

participates in brainstorming ideas

pays more attention to punctuation

points and matches one-to-one with reading

prolific writer

reading performance is below/above/on grade level

reads at grade level

reads beyond the literal meaning

reads fluently, with appropriate expression

reads from a limited selection of books with help

reads with sustained attention

recognizes some conventions of punctuation

recognizes some high-frequency words

recognizes story elements

rereads text to verify and confirm predictions

retells stories

retells story in sequence

selects books to read independently

selects challenging material and a variety of reading material independently

self-corrects if reading makes no sense

sequences events

shares increased awareness of new words

should proofread work for spelling mistakes

stories lack sequence of events

understands cause and effect

understands environmental print

understands literal meaning of text with simple
structure

uses a balance of cues and self-corrects

uses context and own experience to predict

uses context to predict/confirm word/story events

uses environmental print (signs, logos)

uses extensive vocabulary

uses knowledge of oral and written language to
predict

uses letter/sound strategies to generate new words

uses picture clues

uses reference material independently

uses reference materials to locate information with
guidance

would like to see him/her use more sentence variety

writes high-frequency words independently

writing contains interesting or descriptive words
and ideas

writing includes details and examples

writing lacks logical sequence and development

writing needs to be better organized

writing shows inadequate paragraph development

Appendix D: Time Savers

Math: Useful Phrases

adds three 2-digit numbers mentally

applies problem-solving skills

can count to ___

can interpret data using tables, charts, and graphs

cannot always explain the processes used to arrive at
solution

cannot complete the task independently

careless computational skills

collects and organizes data

comfortable with basic arithmetic computations

completes and submits homework punctually

computes accurately

concrete learner in math; needs to have physical
models

counts by 3s from any 2-digit or 3-digit number

demonstrates good problem-solving skills

demonstrates understanding of place value

does not complete assignments in the allotted time

does not compute accurately

extends addition and subtraction facts to tens and
hundreds

fails to complete assigned class work

fails to finish independent assignments

follows directions

forgets instructions or directions

gaining more self-confidence

gives up easily

grasps new concepts readily

has a sound grasp of math concepts

has difficulty with fractions and decimals

has shown strong growth

inconsistent effort

is able to create graphs

is able to follow oral or written directions

is able to understand the tasks to be done and
completes them

is beginning to understand the percent concept

is easily distracted

is unprepared for class (work materials)

knows basic shapes

maintaining grade-level achievement

makes careless errors on assignments

math challenges, which require speed, frustrate [him]

measures accurately

must take care to form numbers better

must take initiative to ask questions when unsure

needs close monitoring

needs much guidance to begin solving a complex
problem

needs to improve quality of work

needs to ask for help on instructions or concepts not understood

needs to be self-directed and take more responsibility

plots data on a bar graph

prefers hands-on activities to written work

quick at mental computation

reaches solutions using good math reasoning

reads 3- and 4-digit numbers

reads Fahrenheit and Celsius temperatures

recalls addition/subtraction facts up to 18

recognizes patterns

records and presents reasoning clearly

shows lack of attention to details

solves money/change problems with coins and bills

takes risks

uncertain of math basics

understands addition and subtraction fact families

understands concepts of volume, capacity

understands place value

understands several methods of graphing

understands simple fractions, decimals, and percentages

uses appropriate measuring tools for measuring weight

uses appropriate strategy to find solutions to math problems

uses comparison symbols (< , >, =) correctly

uses estimation skills

works faster under close supervision

Appendix E: Time Savers

Social Studies and Science: Useful Phrases

applies research skills

applies scientific method

applies the scientific process

communicates understanding of concepts effectively

continues to be an active participant in topic discussions

demonstrates understanding of key concepts

develops ideas effectively

did successful research project with partner

displays critical thinking skills

forgets instructions or directions

grasps new concepts and key questions

grasps new concepts readily

has improved knowledge of the impact of global events

is beginning to see relationships between humans and their physical environment

is sensitive to environmental issues

is taking responsibility for citizenship roles in the classroom

locates information and utilizes resource materials

maintaining grade-level achievement

needs to be self-directed and take more responsibility

needs to take initiative to ask questions

participates in class discussions

shows curiosity about the world

shows sustained interest in experimentation with ideas, materials, and equipment

understands and follows directions well

understands and follows directions with some support

uses creative problem-solving techniques

uses magnifiers and thermometers correctly

was very involved and interested in our study of ___ works well in cooperative groups

Appendix F: Time Savers

Active Verbs

achieves	elaborates	listens	retells
analyzes	engages	manages	respects
applies	enriches	manipulates	reviews
approaches	estimates	measures	revises
attempts	exhibits	models	rewrites
attends	expands	modifies	selects
chooses	explores	motivates	self-directs
classifies	expresses	observes	sequences
commits	focuses	perceives	shares
communicates	follows	organizes	sorts
completes	functions	persists	strives
connects	gains	plays	struggles
constructs	generates	practices	summarizes
contributes	handles	predicts	supports
cooperates	identifies	prepares	sustains
counts	illustrates	prints	understands
decides	incorporates	provides	utilizes
deducts	increases	pursues	views
demonstrates	informs	questions	visualizes
determines	inspires	realizes	works
develops	integrates	recognizes	
displays	interacts	represents	
draws	interprets	researches	

Bibliography

Association of Supervision and Curriculum Development Yearbook. *Communicating Student Progress.* Arlington, VA: ASCD, 1996.

Betts, Bambi. *Assessing Student Learning.* The Principals' Training Center for International School Leadership, 1997.

Bridges, Lois. *Assessment: Continuous Learning.* York, ME: Stenhouse, 1996.

Cummings, Carol. *Managing to Teach.* Edmonds, WA: Teaching Inc., 1992.

Drummond, Mary Jane. *Learning to See: Assessment Through Observation.* Markham, ON: Pembroke, 1994.

Farr, Roger, and Bruce Tone. *Portfolio and Performance Assessment: Helping Students Evaluate Their Progress as Readers and Writers.* New York: Harcourt Brace, 1994.

Fiderer, Adele. *35 Rubrics and Checklists to Assess Reading and Writing.* New York: Scholastic Inc., 1998.

Good, T. and J. Brophy. *Looking in Classrooms,* Fourth Edition. New York: Harper & Row, 1987.

Johnston, Peter. *Knowing Literacy: Constructive Literacy Evaluation.* York, ME: Stenhouse, 1997.

Power, Brenda Miller and Kelly Chandler. *Well-Chosen Words, Narratives, Assessments and Report Card Comments.* York, ME: Stenhouse, 1998.

Shafer, Susan. *Writing Effective Report Card Comments.* New York: Scholastic Inc., 1997.

Silver, Dr. Harvey and Richard Strong. *Diversified Instruction and Assessment.* Silver Strong & Associates, Inc. Workshop.

Teaching K-8, Instructor magazines. New York: Scholastic Inc.

Wiggleworks Software. *Teacher's Assessment Guide.* New York: Scholastic Beginning Literacy System, 2000.